Retire Smart, Retire Happy is a wonderful book—it is reality about retirement with the bark off. Those who think they will live happily ever after when they leave their jobs may be disappointed. But the author shows many have found a way to fulfill their lives afterward.

— Helen Thomas, Columnist, Hearst Newspapers; former White House Correspondent for United Press International

This book is a roadmap to a successful retirement. It is a must-read.

— George Kourpias, President, Alliance for Retired Americans, AFL-CIO

Finally, a book to help people turn the inevitable transition of retirement into another opportunity for growth and adventure.

— Gail Sheehy, Journalist; author of *New Passages: Mapping Your Life Across Time* and *The Silent Passage*

Retire Smart Retire Happy

Retire Smart Retire Happy

Finding Your True Path in Life

Nancy K. Schlossberg, EdD

American Psychological Association
Washington, DC

Fifth Printing March 2005
Sixth Printing July 2006

Published by
APA LifeTools
American Psychological Association
750 First Street, NE
Washington, DC 20002
www.apa.org

To order   Tel: (800) 374-2721; Direct: (202) 336-5510
APA Order Department   Fax: (202) 336-5502; TDD/TTY: (202) 336-6123
P.O. Box 92984   Online: www.apa.org/books/
Washington, DC 20090-2984   E-mail: order@apa.org

In the U.K., Europe, Africa, and the Middle East, copies may be ordered from
American Psychological Association
3 Henrietta Street
Covent Garden, London
WC2E 8LU England

Typeset in Minion by World Composition Services, Inc., Sterling, VA

Printer: Sheridan Books, Inc., Ann Arbor, MI
Cover Designer: Naylor Design, Washington, DC
Technical/Production Editor: Kristen R. Sullivan

The opinions and statements published are the responsibility of the authors, and such opinions and statements do not necessarily represent the policies of the American Psychological Association.

Library of Congress Cataloging-in-Publication Data

Schlossberg, Nancy K., 1929–
   Retire smart, retire happy : finding your true path in life/ by Nancy K. Schlossberg.
      p. cm.
   Includes bibliographical references and index.
   ISBN 1-59147-039-0 (alk. paper)
   1. Retirement—Psychological aspects.   I. Title.

   HQ1062.S325 2003
   306.3'8'019—dc21   2003045380

British Library Cataloguing-in-Publication Data
A CIP record is available from the British Library.

Printed in the United States of America
First Edition

Who of us can see, in its entirety . . . [the] path,
Whether in life or art, and who can tell where it will end?
                              —Artist Marc Chagall

Contents

ACKNOWLEDGMENTS   xiii

INTRODUCTION   3

1. **Demystifying Change   13**
    Transitions: A Definition   14
    Riding the Roller Coaster: The Transition
        Process   17
    Coping With the Transition Process: A
        Restatement   23
    Transition Tips   25
    Your Retirement Audit   26

2. **Looking Inward   27**
    Who Am I?   28
    How Will I Live Without Applause?   32
    What Gives Meaning to My Life?   34
    What About Socializing?   38
    What Should I Do With My Time?   40
    What About Income Withdrawal Syndrome?   42

Is My Body What It Was?   47

Transition Tips   50

Your Internal Audit   52

3. Building Relationships   55

Changing Relationships   55

Together in New Ways   59

"Make New Friends but Keep the Old—One Is Silver, the Other Gold"   73

Location, Location, Location   77

Transition Tips   82

Your Relationship Audit   84

4. Discovering Your Path   87

Continuers: More of the Same, but Different   89

Adventurers: Something New   91

Searchers: Looking for Your Niche   95

Easy Gliders: Content To Go With the Flow   98

Retreaters: Giving Up   100

A Combination Path   101

How Does Identifying Your Path Help?   102

Transition Tips   104

Which Retirement Path Is Yours?   106

5. Taking Charge   109

Understanding Transitions   109

Taking Stock of Your Coping Resources: The 4 S System   114

Taking Charge: Making Retirement Work for You   124

Transition Tips   130

Your Resource Audit   132

6. Learning Retirement Lessons   135

Lesson 1: Prepare for Adventure and Surprise   136

Lesson 2: Learn Optimism   137
Lesson 3: Get Involved, Stay Involved   139
Lesson 4: Keep Dreaming or "My Time"   141
Lesson 5: Balance Your Psychological
    Portfolio   143
Lesson 6: Seize Opportunities   145
Lesson 7: Acknowledge Your Emotions   147
Lesson 8: Go With the Flow, Don't Fight the
    Undertow   149
Lesson 9: Plan A—Always Have a Plan B   150
Lesson 10: A Plan for Everyone   151

7. **Looking Forward   153**
Your Retirement Goals   153
Your Expectations   155
Your Own Name for Retirement   157
Your Future   161
Your Future Quiz   162

FINAL THOUGHTS   165

NOTES   169

INDEX   177

ABOUT THE AUTHOR   183

xi

Acknowledgments

As with any book, many contribute, many count. Most important, I thank all those who agreed to be interviewed for this project. I was particularly pleased when many told me how helpful it was to talk about the ways they worked out new lives. People have enormous ingenuity.

Special thanks to Julia Frank-McNeil, senior director of APA Books (American Psychological Association), who felt the book deserved to be published; Judy Nemes, editorial supervisor of APA Books, whose careful reading and comments were enormously helpful; my editor, encourager, and friend Esther Gordon, who was always there when I needed her with excellent suggestions and clarifications; and Betty Bowers, long-time secretary and friend, who arranged the bibliography in APA style—a tedious task!

My newspaper friends, Susanna McBee and Marianne Means of Hearst Newspapers, and Paul Recer, a senior science reporter at the Associated Press, spent time uncovering needed sources. And thanks to Isaac Green, architect and photographer, who took the picture used on the cover.

Many other friends and colleagues helped as I figured out how to frame the issues. I am only mentioning those who made specific contributions to the content of the book, although many others gave support along the way: Ellen Hoffman, Linda Cashden, Nancy Pinson-Milburn, George Milburn, Barbara Jacobs, Stephanie Kay, Gail Levin, Janet McKee, Janice Birk, Bob Niblock, Beryl Raydn, Mickey and Bob Knox, Marcella Rosen Sachs, David Sachs, members of my women's support group, members of the Queen Bee Travel Group, members of the "Committee of Four" luncheon group, and members of my movie club and book club, all of whom provided support as I moaned about how long it took to write such a short book.

Love and thanks to Steve, my husband and best friend, who never lets me give up. And, of course, to my adult children Karen and Mark, who have been remarkably supportive throughout my career. It is to them that I dedicate this book and hope they will continue to have rich lives and, eventually, creative retirements.

Retire Smart Retire Happy

Introduction

An image of retirement is easy to conjure up, thanks to some familiar clichés: A farewell party involving the presentation of a gift certificate, gold watch or engraved plaque; longtime colleagues promising to keep in touch; an invitation to "come back and visit us any time"; the retiree smiling and speaking enthusiastically of finally getting in some fishing, skiing, time with family, or a second honeymoon. Fade out. Pan in again a few months later and we have several possible scenarios: an energized retiree enthusiastically digging into new activities, inspired to engage in new accomplishments, excitedly meeting the challenges of a new lifestyle; or a depressed soul, deprived of work routine and, therefore, unable to figure out how to fill the days, with whom to have lunch, and how to balance the checkbook on a reduced income.

It is clear that work is the centerpiece of our lives. Whether post-retirement life is positive or negative, work almost always defines who we are, where we go each day, how we live, what kind of car we drive, the size of our home, and even the values we honor. For years, we prepared for work and then, on a daily basis, structured our lives around it. What most of us have not prepared for is the end of full-time work, whether it is paid work, homemaking, or raising children. If anything, daily life in our times—with its clearly defined goals, routines, boundaries, and schedules—conditions us to have difficulty adjusting to the flex-time of retirement.

How can this time of life be made rewarding instead of psychologically paralyzing? That is what this book is about. It is this potential that makes retirement—for those who are in reasonably good health with adequate income—a time of challenge, a moving toward instead of a moving from.

As a professor of counseling psychology, I have devoted most of my career to studying transitions. I developed a model that serves as a lens for examining adult transitions, which include everything from the geographical transition of moving to another town or state, the transition of job loss, and the experiences of adults who make the transition to student life by returning to school, among others. But when I distanced myself from my professional routine, it suddenly became clear that, like moving or going back to school, the transition to retirement is a major one that deserves the same type of attention I had devoted to other phases of adult life. I realized it was possible to apply the generic framework I had developed to a fuller understanding of the retirement transitions.

Armed with this background, I thought I possessed a crystal ball. I believed that I had retirement aced. Right? Wrong. I realized that I had to rethink what I had extrapolated from my studies of change. Back at my desk, I reviewed my previous work on transitions. Despite the apparent differences in all the transitions I had studied, I identified many factors that cut across all transitions. Studying my own work helped me deal with my overriding questions: What next? Now what? How will I find my path in retirement?

WHY WRITE A PSYCHOLOGICAL BOOK ABOUT RETIREMENT AND FOR WHOM?

I am writing for all retirees seeking new ways to lead a fruitful life and for prospective retirees, many of whom are destined to feel let down if they do not give some thought to retirement before it happens. Even for those recent retirees who claim they have never been happier, there is an enormous period of adjustment as they move into uncharted territory.

Retirement is *scary*. And why shouldn't it be? So many aspects of our life are suddenly in flux: what time to get up, what to wear, when to take off for a coffee break, where and when to drop the cleaning off (when this is something you used to do regularly on the way to work). It is no wonder people feel discomfort. Retirement changes not only daily routines but also your role as a full-time worker, relationships with co-workers, and, even more important, your very identity. It is difficult, uncomfortable, even depressing, to know who you *were* but not who you *are*. Retirement is like setting sail in a storm, with little sailing experience, toward a hoped-for destination.

Like sex, retirement is something we think we should be able to do easily and well. In fact, there is much bragging about how easy it is. Unlike sex, however, there is no magic Viagra pill to ease the way! Some retirees report lying to friends, saying "I have never been busier; in fact, I don't know how I had time to work." This optimistic picture may aggravate and intensify the unease of those who have not found their new path, making them question why they, too, can't get a life.

Many ask, "How can I find meaning in my life? Will I ever feel excited about the day again?" The answer is *yes*. And that is what this book intends to do—help readers identify the issues, the changes, the discomfort, and come out feeling that they can find their true path in retirement.

This book will be especially helpful to two major groups: (1) those anticipating retirement who want to identify their needs, take stock of their psychological resources, and define life paths that make sense for them; and (2) current retirees who are struggling to understand why they may feel discontented or confused about their lives. The book offers suggestions and appropriate steps needed to change daily routines, the environment, and relationships to ensure a fulfilling life.

Is this necessary, even for people who are or have been highly successful? Apparently so, for the publisher of a newspaper told me, "We need a book like yours. Write it to me, since that is where I will be in a few years. I want to know the retirement story before I live it."

This book reflects the only thing we know for sure about retirees: There is not *one* retirement story, just as there is no single retiree and no single retirement path. Each story differs. For example, one woman said, "I am at sixes and sevens. I don't know what to do with myself now that I am retired." "Hollow" was the phrase someone else used to describe how he experienced retirement. And yet another person, unable to continue work as an editor because of poor eyesight, described retirement as a "string of hours to be counted." On the other hand, Bob, an optimist, saw retirement as an adventure. One of the many men I interviewed, Bob said retirement was filled with surprises. Originally he viewed it as "not a big deal— just another phase of life." Today, four years later, he realizes it was *big*; it was a series of transitions for which he was unprepared. We will hear Bob's story and others as they take risks to make this phase of life happy, meaningful, and productive.

How I Studied Retirement

To learn about the world of retirement, I interviewed 100 men and women from different walks of life, including residents of mobile-home parks, gated communities, and condos; executives from Fortune 100 companies and blue-collar workers. In addition, I assembled four focus groups around each of the major aspects of the retirement transition: leaving work, changing relationships, body, and self. Although these interviews provided a glimpse of retirement from many points of view, I do not make any claims for the universality of my findings.

When I started this project, I was apprehensive about interviewing people about a transition I was personally experiencing. To my amazement, that very situation helped the process work beautifully. Instead of interviewer and interviewee, we became collaborators in trying to understand what was transpiring in our lives. Almost every retiree thanked me and many said the interview had been "therapeutic," probably because we were all in the same boat, struggling to make sense of this time of life. Many of the people I interviewed were in fact having the time of their lives. At one point I thought I should seek out more "unhappy campers," but I decided that using a more random approach to selecting retirees was equally valid. After all, the purpose of this inquiry was not to catalogue the experiences of retirees in some quantitative sense but to learn from those who have arrived at a fulfilling retirement lifestyle. Finally, conducting the research helped me to confront my own retirement dragons and to arrive at some basic truths that I hope will help others as they confront theirs:

- Retirement is a new, untried experience. For many people, it is the first time they have meaningful choices regarding time, space, and mission without a map or script.

- Retirement is a transition like other transitions, which includes letting go of the past and searching for and creating a new life.

- Retirement transitions are difficult because they force us to answer questions we may have thought we'd already answered for the rest of our lives: Who am I? Do I matter? Do I have a focus? How should I spend my time? Am I competent to cope with whatever the future brings?

- Retirement may unexpectedly transform our relationships with colleagues, friends, and neighbors. What may have been predictable and fulfilling relationships may suddenly seem to be "out of sync" if one person retires before his or her partner, or when they retire at the same time but realize they have different agendas.

- Retirement is paradoxical: For some, this new-found freedom can be freeing, for others it engenders anxiety.

- Retirement, like other transitions, results in many surprises, both positive and negative.

- Retirement involves a series of transitions, making it both complicated and exciting.

AN OVERVIEW: WHAT YOU CAN EXPECT FROM READING THIS BOOK

There are many paths you can take to master your retirement. I have identified five different ways that individuals confront retirement. These paths provide a roadmap for (a) those considering retirement—which path to take—as well as for (b) those already there, who may be asking whether they are on the right path. This book will help you to identify your path and even figure out how to change it. Each chapter will move you forward in this process:

Demystifying Change (chapter 1) shares my personal retirement story as a way to illustrate the transition process, which is applicable to all transitions.

Looking Inward (chapter 2) provides a way to understand what's at stake in one's private world during the retirement transition.

Building Relationships (chapter 3) looks at the changes and importance of supports and relationships.

Discovering Your Path (chapter 4) helps you determine which retirement path you want to take.

Taking Charge (chapter 5) shows you how to garner your resources to negotiate your chosen path.

Learning Retirement Lessons (chapter 6) shares wisdom about retirement from all those interviewed, from the literature, and from my own experience.

Looking Forward (chapter 7) helps you assess how you can make retirement work for you.

Final Thoughts (the concluding chapter) consists of my hope for all of us.

Which path will make retirement the time of your life? If there is one lesson I can pass on from researching and writing this book, it is this: The only person who can answer that question is you. And the only person capable of finding your true path in retirement is also you.

I hope this book helps.

1

Demystifying Change

A while ago, when a newspaper reporter called to interview me about a project that dealt with grandparents raising their grandchildren, I was delighted to describe the specifics of how these grandparents were establishing support groups for other grandparents. The interview was lively until the reporter asked, "What is your title?" I almost gagged and was unable to get out the words "Professor Emerita." I fudged and said, "I am consulting, and doing some teaching."

The truth, which I had not yet accepted, was that I had retired. Because of this, I had no idea who I was. I only knew who I had been. It was an awful moment. Now I say with great pride, "I am a retired professor from the University of Maryland."

What is the process that helped me move from gagging to feeling pride? Why, I wonder, does the process of restructuring a life take so long? The answer, I have discovered, is that restructuring involves change, and change—good or bad, expected or unexpected—unsettles our lives, shakes us up, and requires time before we adjust.

Retirement is change, big time. Just as workers change jobs and careers throughout their employment, so retirees frequently change course. "What do I want to be when I grow up?" is a phrase many new retirees use about themselves, half-jokingly. One reason the transition to retirement is difficult for some is because retirement really is not one, but many, transitions. After all, our work gave us an identity and a lifestyle, and even mapped out our interpersonal relationships. Leaving a job involves more than simply ceasing to work.

As a first step in dealing with changes brought on by retirement, it is important to understand transitions in general. I found that all transitions bring up similar issues and reactions. Transitions change our lives by altering our roles, relationships, routines, and assumptions and our reactions shift as we move onto new paths and leave old ones. Our ability to cope with these changes depends on our resources, which change over time.

Transitions: A Definition

Transitions are *events* (like moving, divorcing, or retiring), or *nonevents* (like not being able to retire when you expected, or not having grandchildren). Whether or not your retirement was, or will be, an anticipated event as mine was, or an unanticipated event like

Bob's, when Congress decided to stop funding his agency, or if your expected retirement failed to occur because you could not afford to retire (your *nonevent*), your life will be changed in many ways.

My studies of nonevent transitions reveal that they are often not obvious.[1] A nonevent refers to something you reasonably expect will happen but doesn't. Its absence can change your life. Because nonevents are generally hidden from view, they are not acknowledged, celebrated, or ritualized in any way. The actual parting from a company, your retirement, is an event, often ritualized by the "gold watch." The nonevent—not having colleagues keep in touch as you expected they would, or not getting the wished for part-time job—carries with it no ritual, even though it might be just as significant as the retirement event.

Whether retirement is an event or a series of events, it changes your life in significant ways. Thus, it qualifies as a transition. A helpful way to figure out how large a change retirement has been or will be is to examine your *roles, relationships, routines,* and *assumptions* before retirement and after retirement. The more they are altered, the more you have to adjust to and cope with the transition.

Even in the case of a nonevent retirement—that is, you are unable to retire as you expected—you are in transition. Although your roles, routines, and relationships have not changed because you are still at work in the same job, your assumptions about the way your life would evolve change dramatically. Sometimes when nothing happens, everything changes.

So back to Bob. After Bob's role as a professional working for Congress ended, he struggled until he developed an entirely new professional *role*. As his job ended, so did his work *relationships*, although his network of family and friends remained the same. Later, when he entered massage school, he developed new relationships, with faculty and other students. His *routines* shifted radically. Accustomed to dressing in a suit and tie, working at an office from 8:30 a.m. to 6 p.m., and coming home with a briefcase full of work, as a student he dressed casually, without a tie and jacket, and developed new routines conforming to his school schedule. Finally, Bob's *assumptions* about himself and the type of lifestyle he wanted changed dramatically. He was no longer the "Washington super worker" type but a more relaxed, introspective person.

As Marlene, a retired office manager, wrote,

> We are now in different worlds. My *relationships* with those who were significant during my working years, have changed. I no longer see many of those I used to see on a daily basis. Instead, I see my husband during the day—something that rarely happened before. My *routines*, including what to wear, when to get up, how to structure the day, are entirely different. I dress in casual clothes most of the time. My schedule no longer has regularity to it. My *role* has changed—from overwhelmed administrator to underwhelmed volunteer. And, of course, my *assumptions* about myself and the world have changed. I never imagined that, yes, there is life after work.

If you have not retired, you might begin to think of the degree to which you expect your life to change. As one woman said, "It is important to think very concretely about what you will do the first day after work ends. It is important to build in structure so you are not at sea." For those already retired, the more your life was altered, the more you have had to adapt.

RIDING THE ROLLER COASTER: THE TRANSITION PROCESS

Adjusting to major transitions takes time, sometimes six months or even a few years. For example, if you interview a person before retirement, during the month of retirement, six months after retirement, and again two years later, you will hear entirely different responses.

What is this process? Is it identifiable? What can you expect as you negotiate retirement transitions? Let's look at the different responses as you move out, move through, and move into a new life.

Moving Out, Letting Go

Leaving a work role can be eased if you remember that your past is not obliterated when you embrace the future. Helen Rose Fuchs Ebaugh, an ex-nun turned sociologist, studied the process of leaving a role.[2] She interviewed former doctors, dentists, police officers, air traffic controllers, teachers, military personnel, athletes, professors, nuns, convicts, prostitutes, and transvestites. She defined the "role exit process" as one in which a person disengages from a role that has been central to that person's identity. The process of ceasing to think of oneself as a dentist, reporter, traveling salesperson, and so forth, is painful for some and a relief for others. She also found that most people who consider leaving a role experience definite periods of letting go: First they experience doubts, then begin to seek alternatives, reach a turning point, and finally identify with a new set of roles.

Your accomplishments and achievements can continue to be sources of pride. Ebaugh wrote, "to become well integrated and a whole person, an ex must incorporate that past history into [the] current identity. Exes, therefore, share the fact that they must establish new identities that incorporate their past social status." Remember, you are still you. Your previous accomplishments can inspire you to achieve along your new path, whether in a part-time or full-time job, on the golf links, traveling, or even baby-sitting for grandchildren.

The ease of letting go of a past role depends on the degree to which it was central to your identity. Clearly, my role as a professor of counseling psychology was central to my sense of self. Letting go of that, and having nothing to go to, created a vacuum. Friends warned that I would flunk retirement because I do not play bridge, tennis, or golf. I had been very committed to my work, much of which dealt with the subject of change. I was considered an expert! Integrating that knowledge into my retired lifestyle, I began researching and writing this book. In addition I put the knowledge to personal use. I talked myself into believing that I could deal with ambiguity, that I love not knowing exactly what I will do, where we will live, how we will live. I began looking forward to the future.

Moving Through: Searching

The struggle of emotionally disengaging from the past is completed when individuals begin to identify themselves in their present roles. For Stan, it was relatively easy to begin thinking of himself as an artist rather than a reporter, because he had been a Sunday painter. For years he had looked forward to the day when he could take his painting seriously. Though he was delighted to have the time to paint, it took him several years to change his self-description from reporter to artist.

Disengaging takes time. For some retirees, time brings adjustment. For others, just the opposite may happen. Research indicates that those who voluntarily retire experience an immediate satisfaction, stemming from the lack of pressure. However, over time, unless the retiree is well motivated and self-directed, there may be unstructured, empty days causing ups and downs. This vacuum is a period of neither-here-nor-there, during which you are relinquishing one set of roles, relationships, routines, and assumptions, and struggling to figure out "what next." Often some of this period is used for grieving for what was and confusion over what might be. Some people begin searching for ways to recreate their past, whereas others use this period as a "moratorium," a time of being suspended between what was and what is to come.

My husband and I decided to move to Sarasota, Florida (where we had vacationed for years) soon after I retired. We were excited, but found the in-between phase long and difficult. On the first Saturday night in our new community, a friend invited us to a dinner party. The group, all of whom lived permanently in Sarasota, was lively and interesting. The hostess toasted our arrival in Sarasota and asked all of the guests to tell us their stories. They were eye openers.

A former cardiologist had volunteered to help teach in the biology department of a local college. At first, they let him run a projector. It took three years before he was invited to lecture and finally to teach. His wife, a former foundation employee, told us she enjoyed tennis and reading, and that she participated in the arts council. Another guest, a retired architect, now studied welding and had designed their house. His wife, a former TV personality, played tennis and actively participated in the Community Foundation. Although it had taken a minimum of two years to feel part of the community, they were all very happy in Sarasota, and felt their lives were meaningful and full.

Their advice: *You must have patience. Give it time.*

I left the dinner party feeling we had met terrific people, all of whom I would love to see again. But I felt frustrated. I didn't want to spend two years before feeling connected. Where, I wondered, do you get patience pills?

After two years, I was still searching. I am a doer and self-starter, yet found nothing to sink my teeth into. Why, I wonder, can't I get it together? Get a passion? A mission? As they say, "Get a life." In addition, my husband developed some health problems, underscoring the point that coping with retirement requires dealing with many transitions simultaneously.

Someone recently asked how to deal with the need for patience. I think it helps to know that transitions take time, that there is no shortcut, and that, in most cases, there will be an eventual resolution.

Moving In: Creating a New Life

I received a call from a woman who had read an article in the paper about my past work and future plans to write a book on retirement. She explained that she had recently moved to a retirement community where it was taboo to discuss the negative aspects of retirement. She felt guilty because she was living the "American Dream," but had not found life meaningful. She had been unable to create a life that was satisfying, and was hoping a book could help her.

I advised her that creating a life takes time. This lesson was borne out by a retired lab technician who had worked in a medical center. After the death of his wife, he began to feel that his life had no purpose.

He had depended on her to organize their social life and now found it difficult to make friends. Alone and bored, depression set in. Realizing that only he alone could pull himself out of it, he spent six months scouting the area for activities and places that might pique his interest. A chance visit to an aquarium attached to a marine laboratory opened an avenue of opportunity. He established a new role for himself as a volunteer researcher at the lab. Using many of his previous interests and skills, the new role simply packaged them in a new way.

In my own life, things finally began to gel for me. I joined several boards and committees, became president of a national professional association, increased my consulting activities, and began making more friends. Some days I feel as busy as when I worked—but now it is without a secretary or paycheck. I am pleased to be involved and serving some useful functions. But I do not want to lose sight of the fact that I am retired! I am here to enjoy the sun, beach, nature, dinners out, theater, and more. Now, it seems I am facing the same problem I had at other times in my life: finding a balance between family, husband, work, volunteering, and social life.

Creating a life structure was the subject of psychologist Daniel Levinson in his landmark book, *The Seasons of a Man's Life*.[3] Although he focused on young adult men creating a life structure, a person who retires from his or her major work activity faces a similar task.

And, as in the young adult's life, once the structure is created, it is not cast in stone forever.

As we have seen, creating a new set of *roles, relationships, routines,* and *assumptions* takes some time. How to structure where you spend your time and where you invest your energies are questions, concerns, and opportunities people share as they create a new life. It is comforting to realize that if one path does not work, there are others, and you can enjoy some new scenery on the way.

COPING WITH THE TRANSITION PROCESS: A RESTATEMENT

Although each individual reacts in a unique manner to retirement, there is a common structure to these reactions. As we have pointed out, most people search for new ways to organize their time. For some, this is a process that leads to new activities; for others there is sadness for what one left. Retirees face different issues as they move out, through, or into new roles (see Table 1.1).

As one leaves work— a phase I refer to as *moving out*—the task is to let go. Let me give an example. A woman who resigned as director of her organization agreed to stay on as a volunteer. Unfortunately she could not let go, and tried to micromanage the activities of her replacement. The newly retired woman needed to acknowledge her regrets about leaving (even though it had been her choice) and grieve for her lost role before she could move on.

TABLE 1.1. The Retirement Transition Process

Phase of retirement	Tasks for retiree	Ways to ease the transition
Moving out	Letting go of your work role	Name the process—grieve
Moving through	Searching for a new way to organize your life	Relabel—Retirement moratorium; Suspend decision making
Moving in	Creating your new path	Reinvest in new activities

After people have left their major activity and before they have found something else absorbing—the transitional phase I call *moving through*—they often are engaged in searching behavior, trying this, then that. One way to deal with that period is to label it differently. Instead of feeling that you are at sea, label the period "your retirement moratorium." During this period, one suspends making any lasting decisions, giving oneself permission to explore. Of course, there are those who immediately move into a new activity without this searching behavior.

Eventually, you will begin creating a new life—a phase I call *moving in*—investing in new activities, establishing new roles, routines, relationships, and assumptions about the new world you are in—the world of retirement. It might not be until this phase that you realize you have chosen your true path.

Transition Tips

☞ **Tip 1.** **Be patient.** Transitions take time. They are like a trip. You fantasize about the trip, you plan the trip, you take the trip, and you remember the trip. Do not be dismayed if, during this process, your reactions shift. Some days you might feel elated, other days depressed.

☞ **Tip 2.** **Understand your change.** The larger the transition, the more your routines, roles, relationships, and assumptions are altered. In a room full of new retirees each one's experience will differ. For some, every part of life is altered. They leave work, move to another city, and begin to see themselves differently. For others, the change is not as big because they stay in the same residence, the same city, and work part time in their organization. You will be able to gauge your adjustment process—the larger the change, the more the adjustment.

☞ **Tip 3.** **Let go of the past, search for the future, then create your new life.** There are different ways to cope with the transition process, depending on whether you are moving out of your work role, moving through, or moving into retirement. And that is what this book is all about. To start you on your way, take the following *Retirement Audit*. It will give you a reading on where you are as you face retirement.

YOUR RETIREMENT AUDIT

1. Where are you in the retirement process (Check one):

   Moving out of your work role ☐

   Moving through searching for a new role ☐

   Moving into after-work roles ☐

2. Did (or will) your retirement change the following?

   a. roles   Yes   No

   b. relationships   Yes   No

   c. routines   Yes   No

   d. assumptions   Yes   No

3. Overall, is retirement a BIG transition for you? If the answer is yes, *keep reading.*

2

Looking Inward

Retirement—whether it's a part-time or full-time departure from a job—forces us to reconsider almost every aspect of our life. For some, retirement may be a positive transition that offers increased life satisfaction and the realization of long-held dreams. For others, retirement may be so stressful that it actually threatens physical and emotional health, provoking vulnerability, a sense of loss, and depression. Checking out these issues is an important step as you creatively cope with retirement.

Gradually for some, suddenly for others, retirement confronts us with a host of decisions—when to actually retire, how to spend our time, where to go each day, even where to live. According to Al Hunt's report in *The Wall Street Journal*, 23% of the retirees surveyed miss their jobs and are concerned about loneliness and being cut off from groups, another 19% are worried about poor health, 10% are concerned about finances, and 7% fear boredom.[1] The retired see this period as a time to enjoy friends and family, but worry about being "has-beens." The boomers expect to have a more activist agenda and to keep working at least part time, and many older boomers expect to spend many hours volunteering. Of course, the pattern will depend on the economy. Some will keep on working as long as possible.

Wherever you are in the retirement process, you need to conduct a reality check on how retirement is affecting your inner life.

WHO AM I?

The issue of identity is critical as you negotiate any transition, but it is especially important during the retirement process. The *Random House Dictionary of the English Language, the Unabridged Edition* defines identity as the "state . . . of remaining the same . . . under varying aspects or conditions." Retirement is a qualitatively different condition from our previous life. Although there is continuity with the past, leaving behind the work that has filled such a major part of our daily life forces us to formulate a new answer to the question "Who am I?"

As an example, a group of women who refer to themselves as "The Retirement Group" meet monthly to discuss their reactions to retirement. All of them had long careers, some in the government, others in education, the arts, business, and homemaking. All agree that the biggest issue they face in retirement is the question of identity. It has taken several years for most of them to feel comfortable without being identified primarily by their former jobs or careers.

The Retirement Group discussed the following questions at great length: Do you have a calling card? If so, what should it say? One woman had a card with several titles while she was working. After retirement, while searching for a new niche, she carried a card with only her name. After two years, she realized she had become a consultant in her area of expertise, so she designed a card reflecting the new identity. Clearly, a card, for those who use them, can be the metaphor for one's vision of an evolving self.

This problem of identity can be especially painful for someone who has become accustomed to working in a powerful position, with staff and other resources for support. For example, a CEO of a major international organization was accustomed to having his staff make his travel arrangements. After retirement, he was suddenly on his own to make airline reservations, keep track of his passport, hotel reservations, and so forth. When a passport clerk asked who he was, the retired executive replied, "I know who I *was*, but not who I *am*." He repeated this story with sadness. When he retired, he had lost both the support of staff and the prestige of his work—an important part of his identity was gone.

Similarly, a woman whose sole occupation had been homemaker functioned like a CEO of a small family business. She fed her husband and four children, arranged their family and social life, maintained their home, and managed their finances. She was lost when their fourth child moved away. She no longer had PTA, baseball, soccer, or dance recitals to attend. Like many former CEOs, she was at a loss.

The searching that many retirees experience, the trial and error of creating a new identity, is reminiscent of a young adult's search. However, this can be especially frustrating because retirees have an expectation that they should know who they are; after all, they have grown up. Nathan Billig, former director of Geriatric Psychiatry at Georgetown University Medical School and author of several books on aging, pointed out that retirement can trigger depression, especially for those whose work was central to their identity.[2] It is obvious that the greater a person's work commitment, the greater the "loss" when that role disappears.

Many reject the identity as retiree because negative labels are often applied to the word—labels such as "over the hill," and "out of the loop." One man confided to me, "I never want people saying they have to take old Bill out to lunch." Psychologists Judith Rodin and Christine Timko argue that negative labels are often internalized, making people behave in ways that suggest they are less competent, less in control—in fact, "over the hill."[3]

The phrases "grumpy old men," "out to pasture," "it's all downhill after 60," reflect societal stereotypes common in the United States and other industrialized nations. These negative labels can become self-fulfilling. One woman realized she was wearing "old lady shoes," and walking as if she were in pain. With the help of a physical therapist specialist, she stood up straighter and began to dispel these negative labels. One man paid particular attention to spots on his clothes. He said it was too easy to fall into the stereotype of the retiree with nothing to do who wore soiled clothes and walked like an old man.

The loss of an institutional identification became clear during a focus group discussion with a number of retired World Bank employees. Regardless of their particular job, the Bank conferred status on these employees. As one man said, "When you say I work for the World Bank, people look at you with respect. When you say 'I am retired,' their eyes glaze over."

It is important to point out that many retirees are proud of their new status and do not experience an identity crisis. Adam and Alice know who they were— highly skilled physicians who had devoted decades to their work—and who they are now—retirees who want to make the most of this time. Alice retired at age 55 from her role as founder and head of a women's health center at a major university. Adam, who headed the psychiatry department of a major university, followed a year later. They adapted quickly and easily. Although the outside world still viewed them as physicians, they decided not to work in medicine, either as volunteers or professionals. Instead, they moved to New Mexico and began traveling to spend time with their three sons and many grandchildren, to play tennis, and to engage in a fulfilling social life. They are content with retirement—neither searching nor retreating. They do not see retirement as negative.

Whether content or confused, your identity is clearly an important issue during retirement.

How Will I Live Without Applause?

We all love to be noticed, recognized, and made to feel we matter. "Applause" is a metaphor for this kind of reinforcement, which, ideally, we received from our work. In fact, the late sociologist Morris Rosenberg suggested that "mattering is a motive: The feeling that others depend on us, are interested in us, are concerned with our fate . . . [and this] exercises a powerful influence on our actions."[4]

Do we believe that we count in others' lives, loom large in their thoughts, and make a difference to them? Do those retirees who feel they matter to society at large, to an institution, and to other individuals adjust more easily than those who feel forgotten, marginalized, or ignored? Rosenberg postulated that the feeling that you matter, that others need you, is crucial for your mental health.

Are there new ways to "matter" in the years after leaving the workplace? Can you "matter" by perfecting your golf game? By volunteering to help others? By strengthening relationships with friends and family? By creating new projects? The answer will be personal. One woman, a former attorney, now plays golf in a woman's league. She never misses her game and feels she is important to the group. In contrast, another person might see golf as the metaphor for an empty life. There is no right or wrong activity. It is whether the activity—be it knitting, tutoring, gardening, traveling, studying, or working—engages you and makes you feel you are appreciated, noticed, and needed.

I believe in, and my research has borne out, the importance of the concept of mattering. The story of a man named Art is an example. In his seventies, the father of three, a successful architect and real estate developer, he moved to Seattle. He and his wife, Bea, decided they "did not want to die in Little Rock"; they wanted to live in an urban area by the water. The move did not turn out as expected.

Art wanted to continue working, but he did not want to start a new practice. On the other hand, he felt he was too old to work for someone else. Calls he made to architects went unanswered. This was particularly shocking, because in Little Rock he had been highly regarded and much sought after for advice.

Art spent several years trying to find a new role as an architect. Half the time he was hopeful; the other half he was discouraged. He continued to dress every day as if he were still working. It took five years and a series of intermediate steps for Art to establish a role, an identity, and a sense that he mattered. He became an active member of his condo board, respected as a technical expert on building maintenance and repairs. He then opened a small office where he did some architectural drafting (mostly for himself), and some photography. He and his wife became extremely involved in the cultural life of the city—taking courses, visiting museums, and seeing plays and movies.

When I asked Art to review the entire experience of the past seven years in terms of his professional life, he drew a graph indicating that he rated high on mattering before moving from Little Rock to Seattle, then went down dramatically and gradually has been moving up. In other words, he has never achieved the level of "mattering" that he had before retirement. He said, "When I die, my death will not leave a gaping hole in my profession, whereas it would have in Arkansas." Clearly, it matters to matter.

WHAT GIVES MEANING TO MY LIFE?

Although retirement, ideally, gives us free time to think about what is important in life, the truth is that we really need to sort some things out beforehand. One person who is doing so is Dee, a baby boomer who knows retirement is the next big step. She and her husband have two adolescent children, an aging mother needing care, and they work hard in a successful business they started. Recently, she began to reflect on her life, where she is, and where she is going. She started taking time for herself, is losing weight, and is attending church every Sunday with her daughter. All of this indicates that she is paying attention to herself—her body, soul, finances, and other matters. She knows her life will not always be as full of responsibilities, and she is thinking ahead to that time.

Presumably, if all of us had taken the time to attend to ourselves, we would not find ourselves feeling as Donald does. Donald, who retired as CEO of a major corporation when he was 68 years old, called retirement "the most traumatic event of my life." He used the word "hollow" to describe his experience. Pounding on the table, he demonstrated, "This is solid; hollow is empty. That's what retirement is. You can only golf, fish, or play tennis so many hours."

After his retirement Donald served in leadership roles in the nonprofit world. Despite his continuing contributions, he realized that he was not prepared to leave his major work. Although he is looking, he has no "zest" for anything. Donald represents those who are creative and extremely competent, but who are unable to regain a sense of mission. They need to reexamine priorities and to understand the need for renewal of the body, mind, and soul so that when work is less prominent their lives will still be full.

At the other end of the spectrum is my husband, Steve. As a young man, he shocked his family by leaving his job as manager of a women's dress store to become a labor organizer. Living in a small southern town where racial prejudice was rampant, he had been living a divided life. During the day he managed the store, but at night he worked for racial, social and economic justice with like-minded friends. Steve subsequently left what his family viewed as a promising career for what they considered to be a fly-by-night job for a union. But meaning through work was critical to Steve. Over the years, he went on to become a labor lawyer and then general counsel of a major union. His life had purpose—his mission was to level the playing field between workers and management. Now retired, Steve retains his sense of purpose by staying involved with the labor movement. He lectures on the history of labor, serves on several boards, and continues consulting with a group that is organizing professionals.

Another fortunate retiree is Myrtle, who worked for 40 years as a practical baby nurse. It took some time, but she also was able to translate her sense of purpose from her active work life into her retirement. Myrtle loved caring for babies, and over the years kept in touch with most of the families for whom she had worked. When poor health forced her to retire, she felt useless. Then, through the intervention of a career counselor, Myrtle restored purpose to her life by becoming an at-home phone volunteer for a nearby hospital. Her job, to call patients after they leave the hospital to check on their well-being, helped her regain meaning in her life.

Throughout my research, I heard stories of retirees' rekindled interest in spirituality. And though there are many definitions of spirituality, the one that seems most applicable is the search for meaning and mission in life. Julia's life fell apart when her second husband became critically ill and her granddaughter was born with a major disability. Then Julia's path of self-discovery began. She started seeing a therapist who helped her deal with her family situation. Next, she reported, "I began hiking and mountain climbing—activities designed to help me find peace and answers. I tried lots of healing methods. I went to a bookstore and stood in front of the self-help section and was drawn to a book that introduced me to the spiritual world. The book spoke to me. I then sought out others who shared this particular spiritual approach. I became involved in the life of their community. I refused to be a victim." Now Julia keeps logs every evening, meditates, reads, and sees herself as someone "with a limitless source of strength."

We know that spirituality and religion are not the same. However, both have become increasingly significant in many people's lives as they grow older. Harold Koenig, a psychiatrist at Duke University Medical Center, studied 4,000 men and women and found that religion was a great comfort, a coping mechanism, a center for social life, and a way to make meaning out of life.[5] This finding was echoed in an article by Winifred Gallagher in *The New York Times*: "Just as young adults look to their work to help define their identity, older adults facing a new phase of life—retirement—increasingly regard religion as an important means of redefining who they are."[6] The Kauslers, who study aging, estimate that well over 50 percent of older people pray on a daily basis.[7]

Building on this increased interest in religion and spirituality, reporter Mary Duenwald pointed out that a number of medical schools now teach future physicians how to address patients' religious and spiritual needs.[8]

However, the debate continues about the connection between participation in religious activities and improved health. For example, Duenwald reported that Koenig sees such a connection whereas others, like Dr. Richard Sloan of Columbia University, find no evidence connecting religious beliefs to better health.

After many interviews, I concluded that people define spirituality in different ways, but the common theme is that people are paying attention to their inner life. Clearly, this can be helpful and provide comfort as you negotiate the retirement transitions.

WHAT ABOUT SOCIALIZING?

A retired professor pinpointed one of the important changes that can occur in retirement: "Suddenly you are on your own." In his department, everyone would come early to work to chat. He missed this easy camaraderie and asked, "Now that I'm retired, with whom do I schmooze?"

Melanie had a similar experience. As a key manager in a travel agency for many years, she had felt essential to the company's operation. When her husband decided to retire, she decided that the "right thing to do" was for her to retire also. After taking a vacation to the Outer Banks of North Carolina and spending some time gardening and visiting with family, Melanie expressed ambivalence about her decision. Unable to define the problem, she simply felt emptiness in her life. The worst part was her anger at herself for not adjusting. As we talked, it became clear that she had neither acknowledged nor mourned her loss of camaraderie. She did not miss her work; she missed her workplace.

As we give up a paycheck we also give up structured companionship or "social capital." Articles and books on retirement pay much attention to ways to replace financial capital, but few focus on ways to replace psychological or social capital. To this end, sociologists Phyllis Moen and Vivian Fields studied people ages 50–72 who leave their primary work and are receiving pensions.[9] They concluded that work provides the principal source of "social capital" in America. For retirees, they found, unpaid community participation—volunteer work—served as an effective substitute. Those retirees who are working or engaged in their communities will undoubtedly have a better quality of life than those who withdraw or retreat.

This underscores what we know: Work furnishes a sense of place and membership in a valued community. This sense of place and belonging in turn provides individuals with feelings of worth. As we saw in chapter 1, when someone leaves a major role—in this case the worker role—one goes through a period of searching for a new sense of worth and a place in a new social community. For many, this is a period with no roadmap, when one is part of neither the work world nor the retirement world.

Although we are encouraged to spend time figuring out the financial resources we'll have after retirement, much less attention is paid to figuring out the equally significant aspect of post-retirement life—social capital. Retirees need both. And it is essential that every retiree address the question of how to receive enough social as well as financial capital. This can be accomplished in a number of ways—participation in part-time work, community activities, learning, or fun leisure pursuits. Each person's menu will differ.

You may find continuing your education to be a great way to increase your social capital. Herb worked hard and finally sold his business. He suddenly found himself asking a lot of questions. What to do? Where to go? With whom to talk? Herb went to school, completed his BA, and is now writing his master's thesis. Others who are not as academically ambitious can take courses sponsored by Elderhostel. Also, many universities sponsor academic programs where retirees teach other retirees. This learning and education in a hospitable setting provides a vehicle for obtaining social capital and also a way to answer the next section's question.

WHAT SHOULD I DO WITH MY TIME?

The routine of getting up in the morning and working on a schedule provides a pace and structure to the week, the month, the year. Interviews with new retirees reveal a common concern about their "life structure"—what to do the first day, week, or month after the last day of work. A former World Bank executive avoided being at loose ends by planning exactly what she would do the first day—what she called the "R" day. Her approach suggested that she would make similar efforts to plan out a good part of the subsequent days and weeks as well. In contrast, another retiree reported, "I wake up now, throw on a house dress, and start wandering around the apartment. Before, I always got up, made coffee, dressed, quickly did the dishes and rushed to the metro. Now it takes me all morning to clear the breakfast table and get dressed. And often my dressing is aimless. Am I just going to be home, go shopping, or visit the grandchildren?" Another person, who had been retired for two years, said, "I miss Saturdays . . . every day is similar and I miss the break from weekday to weekend."

People's perception of time varies. Some retirees feel that they're very busy. Over and over I heard, "I am so busy. I don't know how I ever had the time to work." When I asked a retired journalist what he meant by that, he said, "We are now busy with the bureaucracy of living." Another friend related, "I can't quite put my finger on it but I am very busy. Sometimes I think I want to return to work, but then I realize I would not have the time."

For others, days pass slowly. Sue, the retired manager of a small retail store, reported, "In the past, I felt that I had to get to work, no matter what the weather. Today there was snow, and I started to clean off the car. Suddenly I realized, there was no need to go out in snowy weather."

I became curious. Are retirees busier than ever? What do retirees mean when they say, "I don't know how I ever had time to work." John P. Robinson, sociologist at the University of Maryland, conducts periodic surveys to identify ways Americans spend their time.[10] In 1995, Americans over age 65 said they had 7 more hours of free time than their retired counterparts had reported 10 years earlier.

How do these retirees spend their time? The activities included housework, television, volunteer work, increased social life, and a more leisurely pace with the routines of daily living. According to Robinson, they increased their television viewing by about 50 percent and spent more time devoted to housework, visiting with family, and volunteer work.

Some retirees respond negatively to the new freedom of time, whereas others see it as a positive change. One person wrote, "Another surprise about retirement was that I suddenly had a lot more control over how I spent my time. Until then, almost all my time belonged to my job, mostly because I was something of a workaholic." Retirees who report that they are "busier than ever" tend to have an upbeat feeling about their lives. But those who have time on their hands are often depressed and feel that life is not meaningful anymore.

WHAT ABOUT INCOME WITHDRAWAL SYNDROME?

Newsweek columnist Jane Bryant Quinn wrote, "For many boomers, there are two pressing questions: When can I retire, and how do I pay those stiff tuition bills?"[11] The answers to these questions will determine when and if a person retires.

The media trumpet a constant message that Americans are not saving enough for retirement, and the statistics on the number of retirees who live on the economic edge are sobering. It's no wonder that pre-retirees and retirees alike seem to be suffering from "income withdrawal syndrome." Two investment officers, one at a bank and one at a brokerage house, told me that even their clients with more than adequate income become anxious when they retire and no longer receive a regular salary check.

Contrast John, a former automobile worker whose pension enabled him to retire to a life of leisure, with Don, a retired tool and die worker, who has no retirement benefits except social security because he did not work in a union shop. Forced to retire because of health, Don feels he is on the edge financially. Fortunately he supplements his income by working part time driving people to the airport. This extra money makes the difference for him. He knows that he will eventually need to give up driving. He is age 80 and has serious back problems.

Fortunately, there are hundreds of books that outline ways to assess your financial resources. Ellen Hoffman, writer on the financial aspects of retirement, reviewed the sources of potential income and the amount of retirement income needed (the conventional wisdom is 70% of pre-retirement income).[12] She warned, "A mistaken decision to leave work before you're ready can be remedied, but some forethought about why you're taking early retirement could save you time and money." Her book provides tips for your financial security, even if you waited until you retired to pay attention to this subject.

Financial assets are objective in that one has a certain amount of money, and subjective in one's assessment of one's financial resources. Many companies run pre-retirement programs that focus on how much money an individual can expect from various sources. How does an individual assess financial resources? Most retirees compare their financial resources with what they had when they worked. Some see their resources as better than before, and others see them as just the same or much less than before.

For example, Sarah was six months away from retirement and preoccupied with what her income would be. Would she be able to afford to move to a new city? Did she have to sell her home or should she rent it? What could she afford? Her accountant explained that with her pension and Social Security she would be almost as well off as when she earned a salary. Actually, she doubted the truth of what the accountant said and was afraid to move ahead on her plans.

James, 70 years old, would love to retire and move to the beach full time. However, he is continuing to work many different jobs and is afraid to retire because he needs the money. He has a house, Social Security, but no pensions. He feels trapped. Contrast that with Bill and Gina, whose sources of income diminished considerably with retirement, yet they optimistically reported, "We can continue to live as comfortably as when salaried—and a lot happier." The absence of salary has been balanced by a philosophical adjustment to saving and spending habits. They no longer feel they must build a huge financial windfall for their grown children and grandchildren. They moved further out from the city so that housing would be less expensive. Their spending habits have changed; they have fewer clothing purchases and big-ticket items. "One car is enough," they decided. Others in their situation would evaluate the diminished income as depressing. In the long run, it is the individual's perception of income, and of how the income fits with his or her identity. For some, giving up a second car would indicate downward mobility. Bill and Gina's new lifestyle was a collaborative decision.

I interviewed Rose, who felt diminished and sad. "All my life I have had to worry about making ends meet. I worked hard and felt that Social Security would take care of everything. Actually, it barely covers my cost of living, and I have no other sources of income. I am dependent on my children for help."

Income does change with retirement and it certainly influences the way one lives, one's assumptions about oneself, and one's comfort level. Psychologists Richard Lazarus and Susan Folkman provided a framework for understanding your approach to any major change.[13] The key is your evaluation of the change. In the case of a change in your retirement income, ask yourself is the change positive, benign, or negative? Then evaluate your resources for coping with your changed financial situation. Even if you feel it is less than desired, do you feel that you can make it, live a good life, and not be consumed with what-ifs such as, "What if I had saved more? What if I had taken advantage of deferred income? What if I had invested more wisely and diversified my portfolio?" Your evaluation, then, has two parts: evaluating the financial situation itself and your personal and psychological resources for coping with the situation.

Rose was depressed because she saw her reduced income as frightening. Furthermore, she did not feel she had the emotional resources to cope with this. Juanita saw the changed market as negative, and her reduced income as negative. However, she knew that she had the inner resources to cope. She decided to sell her large apartment and move into a smaller one. She became excited at this prospect. Instead of evaluating the necessity to downsize as negative, she saw it as an opportunity to redecorate and live in a cozier place.

It may be important to keep in mind that money is not the ultimate source of happiness in retirement. For example, a former CEO of a Fortune 100 company whose income alone approached one million dollars found that money did not buy happiness. He had all the money he could possibly need but was missing out on other things.

In summary, it is usually not so much the objective income that matters, but your perceptions about how the income will affect your life and how to cope with these changes. Financial health has a subjective as well as objective component. "Income withdrawal syndrome" seems inevitable at first. But over time it is important to take a realistic inventory of where you are, what resources you have, and how your resources and goals match up. A financial planner can help you figure out how to handle your specific situation.

IS MY BODY WHAT IT WAS?

It is clear that satisfaction with retirement is associated with good health, however it is defined. Most of those interviewed saw health in broad terms, including mental and physical health, a healthy soul, and a healthy living environment. There were conflicting views about the degree to which older people can take control of their health. On one hand, there is great optimism about the extensive use of health clubs, trainers, and exercise. On the other hand, *The New York Times* health columnist Jane Brody wrote that despite the impression that older people have made significant improvements in their activity levels, 40% are still sedentary. According to Brody, only 15% of Americans engage in moderate physical activity for 30 minutes 5 or more times a week, despite the fact that "participation in regular physical activity is the one behavioral change that can have the greatest impact on health and longevity."[14]

Attitude clearly influences one's ability to cope with health problems. Two women may have the same diagnosis, but if one is a pessimist and the other an optimist, the optimist will assume a positive outcome to taking care of herself and the pessimist will assume the worst and become even sicker. Returning to the work of Lazarus: People assess their health situation as either positive, negative, or benign. At the same time, they assess their resources for coping with their health situation.

Back to the retirement group of women mentioned earlier, most of whom are in good health and all of whom are active in work or volunteer activities, the conversation inevitably returned to fears about aging. Their fear is related to the possibility of their own diminishing health. Exacerbating these fears is the assumption that they will probably spend a number of years as widows. They anxiously ask themselves questions: What would they do? Where would they live? Who would take care of them? Their concerns are echoed in the song of folksinger Joe Glazer, "Who will take care of you, how'll you get by, when you're too old to work and too young to die."[15]

Retirement brought on by health problems need not be a negative event. Consider this story about such a retirement. A degenerative disease triggered Paula's retirement. Her husband decided to retire, too; they wanted to be together, travel, and make the most of the time while she was still somewhat mobile.

Paula described her degenerative disease with grace, humor, and depth. She made it clear that this disease would affect her ability to walk and even her control of her bodily functions—in short, this disease would change her life. Her question was whether she would let this disease consume her mind and soul as well as her body. Her answer: A resounding *no*.

They moved close to their son, daughter-in-law, and grandchildren. They thought long and hard about the move. It was a new location "where we had no history, no 'official' way to make contacts, thereby depending upon our son and daughter-in-law for making contacts."

Six months after they moved, I asked how she felt about her new life. She responded, "Still very positively. My husband and I take our 'dipstick' reading every three months. We see how things are progressing. It's surprised us how satisfied we both are." She added that their routine had stabilized, they had met many new friends, and they had become active in their church.

She continued, "I work at being a retiree, just as I did when I had career responsibilities. My choice for retirement is to be fully engaged. I am extremely happy to have more selective control over how my time and energy are to be used. I am really enjoying having more time to spend on my art. My husband and I had to learn to live together 24 hours a day, and this was very positive. We decided we not only loved each other, we really liked each other. We have scheduled work times when we don't interrupt each other, and times when we do things alone. And, we did get two phone lines. . . . Also, we have always found a church home where we can minister to others and be ministered to by the congregation. Our faith has been important to us as individuals and as a couple. Both of us also try to keep our bodies healthy through exercise and diet."

Paula is thankful that they chose to retire. She is amazed at how well her husband has adapted to it and how much they are enjoying this "new adventure." Her physical limitations are clearly a factor. She wrote, "Yesterday I was so mad that my body isn't as strong as it used to be. I had to go to bed all afternoon. My mind and heart are not in bed, but yesterday I was exhausted. I had been at an evening life drawing class. However, I am willing to pay the price for my art." Despite her health problems, Paula said, "I think of retirement not as an ending, but as another transition of life; it is a change that provides another life choice where you can continue to learn and live—with or without total good health."

TRANSITION TIPS

☞ **Tip 1. Look inward.** Take this time to attend to your inner life—your body, soul, and other matters. It is a challenging task to make yours "a life examined," as Paula and others have done. But doing so can help avert problems that crop up continually during the retirement years.

☞ **Tip 2. Make sure you feel you matter.** Assess your life regularly—like Paula, take a "dipstick" of your life. Are you doing things that make you feel appreciated, recognized, and that you matter? If the answer is no, you need to start creatively thinking about how to arrange your life so that you will feel you matter.

☞ **Tip 3. Contemplate what has meaning for you.** Spirituality is an important component of life, and for many people, helps with this new phase of life. The spiritual path differs for each individual—whether it is yoga, reading, or participation in organized religion.

☞ **Tip 4. Replace the relationships you had at work.** Figure out with whom you can "schmooze." It is important to take an active role in building a new network of friends and acquaintances. Joining groups, starting a book group, or taking classes are examples of ways to increase your relationships after work.

☞ **Tip 5. Keep a time diary.** See how and where you spend your time. This will enable you to decide whether or not you need more structure to your days, your week, or your month.

☞ **Tip 6. Build physical activity into your life.** Join a health club, a walking group, get a trainer, or watch exercise tapes geared to your physical ability.

☞ **Tip 7. Keep your financial life on track.** Make use of financial planners, accountants, and good books. To get started with the process of looking inward, you may want to take the following *Internal Audit.*

YOUR INTERNAL AUDIT

Rate the following on a 3-point scale with 1 being "Not at all," 2 being "Somewhat," and 3 being "Very much."

My identity

I am forward looking and do not focus on
who I used to be pre-retirement 1 2 3
I am comfortable with my identity as a
retiree 1 2 3

My feelings of importance to others

I feel I still "matter" to many people and
organizations.................................... 1 2 3
Former colleagues still want to see me
socially... 1 2 3

Life's meaning

I find meaning in my activities now that I
have retired 1 2 3
I get comfort from my faith 1 2 3

My colleague and social quotient

I find plenty of people to talk to and visit
with.. 1 2 3
I am part of one or more groups that meet
regularly... 1 2 3

Use of time

I expect to be as busy as I want during
retirement....................................... 1 2 3
I expect that I will be able to fill my time
with worthwhile activities........................... 1 2 3

Financial resources

I am comfortable with my Social Security
and pensions................................... 1 2 3
I feel positive about my finances 1 2 3

My health

I exercise regularly and take care of myself....	1	2	3
I feel positive about my health	1	2	3

All those items that you marked *1* seem to present problems for you. These are issues you will confront or are already confronting you. These issues should be manageable as you complete the remaining steps to finding your path in retirement.

3

Building Relationships

Lenny, a former assembly line worker for Ford Motor Company, retired after 30 years at age 50 so that he could spend time with his wife while he was still young enough to make love, go dancing, and have fun. To others, all this extra time might lead to conflicts with family and friends. "I never used to see my wife during the day, so we never argued. Now we go grocery shopping together and fight over which brand of cereal to buy. It is ridiculous."

If you are thinking of retiring, now is the time to do a reality check of how retirement might change your relationships; if you are retired, now is the time to check on what's going right and what needs fixing. This is the time to count your assets, and your biggest assets are your relationships.

CHANGING RELATIONSHIPS

Sociologist Robert Weiss found that relationships tend to be specialized in what they provide, and, as a consequence, we need to maintain a number of different relationships for our well-being.[1] As you read this following list, think about the degree to which your relationship needs have changed or will change as a result of retirement.

- The need for *Attachment* is served through relationships that are constant and safe. These usually occur in marriage, partnerships, or very close friendships. Example: Aileen stayed in Harrisburg, her hometown, after she retired and her husband died. The reason? She had close friends there available to her on a daily basis.

- *Social integration,* another important need, is provided by those relationships in which individuals have similar concerns. These usually occur when people work together toward a common goal in work or volunteer settings. To satisfy the need to keep involved with others, many retirees substitute volunteer activity for paid work. Example: Elvis, a former police officer, now volunteers at the Boys' Club; physicians are working as volunteers in senior centers. In fact, volunteerism among retirees has increased substantially over the past few years.

- *Opportunity for nurturance* occurs in those relationships in which we care for friends, family, and children, thus making us feel that we matter because we are needed. You can also seek out places where you can nurture; for example, joining an Adopt-A-Grandchild program. Others find opportunities to nurture that they had not bargained for. For example, there are a growing number of grandparents (over 3 million) raising grandchildren because of some tragedy that befell their adult children. When I asked a group how they felt about the responsibility, they responded, "We have no choice. They need us, and we can provide a safe haven for them."

- *Reassurance of worth* results when our competence is affirmed by the relationships in our family, community, or work. Those who gained a great deal of self-worth from their work, and now feel a vacuum, can receive kudos and heightened self-esteem from volunteer or part-time paid work in the community. Example: Barbara, formerly a lawyer, serves on two working boards and reported, "I am in the 'better world business.' I feel I am doing worthwhile things."

- *Sense of reliable alliance* is assured when we have continuity in our relationships with kin, providing us with a sense of being grounded. Again, this is why retirees choose to spend more time with family and close friends after leaving the workplace. Example: Joyce is thrilled that retirement enables her to visit her adult children and grandchildren whenever the spirit moves her, or whenever there is a family occasion.

- *Obtaining guidance* refers to those relationships that provide advice and counsel when we need it. For those who retire and move to a new state, there is a period of trial and error as they locate new doctors, hairdressers, cleaners, therapists, as well as friends.

Think about how the needs listed here were met and are being met now that you are changing your lifestyle. How do you create the balance needed for a healthy, sound, and fruitful lifestyle? Psychologists Robert Kahn and Toni Antonucci developed a way of visualizing relationships at a given point in time.[2] Identifying your relationships will provide a way of visualizing your potential supports. To do this, Kahn and Antonucci provided a series of concentric circles that they labeled the individual's "convoy of social support." I think of this convoy as a "circle of intimates and acquaintances." The circle closest to the individual in the center includes the individual's most intimate friends and family, who presumably are part of the individual's life forever. These are the people who provide "attachment" and a sense of "reliable alliance." For example, one woman, Elisa, has two sisters. They are her family but also her closest friends. Elisa would put those names in the center circle. On the other hand, Fred and his brother, Ted, do not speak. Fred would not include Ted in the inner circle, or, for that matter, in any circle. Ted is not part of Fred's convoy of social support. It is important to note that there is no magic or "normal" number of people one should include in this inner circle. Clearly, there are individual differences as well as cultural differences in the number of people considered intimate. This group can be very small or large.

The next circle includes family, friends and neighbors—again those who provide attachment, social integration, reliable alliance, and often guidance. These are people very close to the individual in the center, but not those included in the most intimate circle. The circle farthest away represents institutional relationships. These are often colleagues, neighbors, supervisors, and acquaintances—people who will change as your circumstances change.

Comparing your "convoy" before and after retirement provides an easy way to visualize the changes in your relationships: who has left, who is new, where the gaps are. At the end of this chapter, you can see two diagrams that represent these circles of friends and acquaintances. You can do your own personal "relationship audit" by filling in the circles according to the directions given there.

TOGETHER IN NEW WAYS

It is clear that retirement influences the marital or partner relationship: In some instances the impact is positive, in others negative. But whether positive or negative, there is, for most, a major adjustment.

Not surprisingly, men and women may experience retirement differently. As part of the Cornell Retirement and Well-Being Study, Jungmeen E. Kim and Phyllis Moen collected data on 534 married men and women between the ages of 50 and 72 and found that they indeed had different retirement experiences, partly because of their different work histories. For most men, work has been continuous; for many women work has been discontinuous. Women move in and out of the work force more frequently than men. When examining the experiences of couples, we see many retiring at different times. Kim and Moen described the complexities involved when couples retire. Often they are dealing with issues surrounding the loss of two paychecks and the psychological consequences of two phased retirements.[3]

Some Turf Issues

At home together may or may not be cozy. Writer Barbara Matusow[4] reported that many women "secretly dreaded having someone around the house all day, looking over our shoulders, hearing our phone conversations." Who gets to use the phone, fax, computer, or e-mail? One woman found it irritating to always be asked, "Where are you going?" She was accustomed to getting in her car and going. Obviously, these niggling issues are worldwide. The Japanese refer to retirement as the "wet leaves" phenomenon, where women see that men "are as pesky and hard to get rid of as fallen wet leaves." The increase in divorce following men's retirement prompted Yoriko Madoka, a member of parliament, to initiate a support network for women whose husbands have retired. "When their husbands were working they did not see their husband's face all day; now their husband is home for dinner sitting around the table with nothing to say."[5]

Clearly, negotiating is a critical component of marriage. Witness the following case history. Marty retired at age 63 after his company was downsized and he was let go. Devastated, he and his wife, Julia, moved to Florida, where her mother had a condo. At the outset of our interview, they told me how much they enjoyed the sun and beach. After a few minutes they looked at each other and nodded, implying it was OK to tell the truth.

After they had moved, they fought constantly. Julia, used to having the house to herself, hated having her husband "underfoot," especially a husband whom she saw as a failure. The fights escalated, and they knew they needed space. Each took a part-time job: Marty at a restaurant and Julia at a clothing store. This eased the tension. After several years, they stopped working and settled into a routine of golf, cooking, seeing friends, and traveling.

My interviews produced some scenarios that were positive from the outset. The former assembly line worker (previously mentioned), Lenny, and his wife, Cathy, an owner of a small beauty salon, retired at age 50. He had put in 30 years at the plant. They moved to Oregon, and now spend three or four afternoons dancing at various clubs, socializing regularly, watching their diets. Larry claimed, "This is the happiest time of my life. I wanted a chance to be together while we could still enjoy each other." What a change for a couple that always communicated before, but mostly by writing notes!

Even a primarily positive relationship experience post-retirement often may only come after a period of adjustment. Mary retired before she was ready. Her husband, at the top of his form as a surgeon, decided to retire "before his hands began to shake." He also felt he should leave New Jersey and move to a community where he had not been a leader in his hometown, because, if he remained as a retiree, he might feel marginalized. After her initial resistance, Mary became enthusiastic about spending time together—something they had not done since the early days of marriage. They found that they had to get to know each other all over again.

Ann echoed these sentiments. Her husband took early retirement and she looked forward to time together. Soon after retirement, however, she began to miss the former routine—her husband had his life, she had hers, they got together in the evening with the children. They did not know how to act or what to talk about. He resented her "in his space," just as she resented him. She had to "reinvent" herself, she felt, and they had to work out a new routine of being together. Retirement caused the rhythm of their lives to change drastically.

Neither Mary nor Ann wanted to return to their working lives and the responsibilities that entailed. Together with their spouses, they found a new modus operandi. But it took time—three years.

Someone asked me to give some specific ways that couples could accommodate to retirement. There are no easy answers, except perhaps, the same way they accommodated to marriage—hopefully showing respect, kindness, understanding, empathy, and love. Give it time, tell each other what the irritants are, keep communication open, and go to a therapist together if you cannot seem to work it out yourselves.

Out of Sync

At a recent meeting, a group of women began discussing a problem that concerned all of them. One woman reported that she and her husband had never fought until recently. She is still constantly on the go, participating on many boards and committees, and feeling useful and needed. Her husband, on the other hand, sits home watching television or reading. She thinks he should do more, be active, and "get off his duff." Finally he told her that if he did not mind her involvements, why couldn't she let him be?

Several of the other women reported similar concerns. Elaine reported liking this period of her life with time for family and friends. Yet she felt sad, she reported, that her husband could not be more fulfilled. Whereas she is engaged, Milt is a couch potato. The most negative thing is that both of them feel she has become "bitchy"— always nagging, never satisfied with their life or with Milt.

Does gender affect the way an individual reacts to retirement? Clearly, yes. There are several explanations for this gender difference. Because men and women often have been in different work worlds, they will be in different retirement worlds. According to the findings of the Cornell Retirement and Well-Being Study mentioned earlier, men and women have distinct career paths: men's paths showed more stability, whereas women were more varied. Men's careers seemed independent of family, whereas women's were tied to family.

However, psychologist David Gutmann offered another explanation. He found that older men and women experience a "sex-role turnover—that is, men and women 'reclaim' those aspects of themselves that were dormant."[6] For example, men who were "aggressive" and "very masterful" become more nurturing; women who had been involved in family relationships are out the door, wanting to conquer new horizons.

This pattern became clear during a retirement workshop I conducted for a Fortune 100 company that had an unwritten rule that executives (then all men) must retire at age 60. The workshop participants were male executives and their wives. During the discussion, it was obvious that the prospective retirement was affecting the women in ways very different from the men. One woman practically screamed out: "Where were you when *I* was raising *our* children? Now that you are about to retire, you want to plan trips. I finally have found something I want to do—a job I love. And I will not give it up to travel with you. No way!"

Others expressed the same resentment—that they had always played second fiddle to their husband's jobs, that they had given up careers, raised the children alone, and now they were being asked to set aside new careers to be companions to their husbands. Clearly, these couples were "out of sync." As a matter of fact, the headline of an article in *The New York Times* says it all: "She's Wound Up in a Career; He Wants to Wind Down."[7]

Another interpretation is that previously unresolved conflicts put many men and women in retirement on a collision course. Many couples have been too busy during working and child-raising years to work out their relationship. For example, Norm, a musician, retired because of poor health but is now back working with his band part time. He cannot go on trips of more than two hours because of circulatory problems. Stephanie, his wife, says they never saw each other when he was working seven days a week; they still do not see each other. She is angry. Now, with his need for naps and medical appointments taking up the free time between his gigs, they will never do the things she hoped they would do, such as travel. They are not negotiating a new way of life for his semi-retirement years; they are continuing the same pattern of work and anger they have always followed.

But it is always gratifying to know that many couples find this period of being out of step not necessarily a time to become out of sync. For example, Sol is retired and his wife is still working. In fact, she is at the top of her form and in a very responsible position. He does not want her to stop working. In fact, he is concerned about what will happen when his wife retires. He loves the privacy and space.

Speaking of negotiating, it is interesting to note that in a study of 60 couples living in the Boston area, researchers Vinick and Ekerdt found that during the year after retirement, almost all the couples were searching for ways to negotiate household tasks.[8] Those who perceived that there was equity in the arrangement of household tasks rated high on the researchers' Satisfaction Index.

Think ahead to where your potential conflict will be. How will you handle retirements taking place at different times? I suggest trying a trial retirement. Take a month off and see what it is like to be together 24 hours a day. For long-suppressed resentments, this may finally be the time to see a therapist, counselor, psychologist, or social worker. But couples or individuals do not live in a vacuum. They are usually part of larger family constellations: in-laws, adult children, siblings, and even parents now that people live so much longer. Anytime someone in the constellation shifts, the whole system is affected.

Adult Children's Reactions

Adult children have expectations about how their parents should live. When parents' behavior does not mesh with these expectations, troubles arise. Molly, a former housekeeper, married Dale, a widower and former plumber, when they were both in their 70s. They described joy in finding each other. They loved their home, not having to work so hard any more, and having the opportunity to play, go dancing, and just enjoy themselves. However, there was a downside: They both felt terrible about the reaction of Dale's adult children to the remarriage. Molly, a very outgoing and giving person, tried to please them, cook for them, welcome them. Both she and Dale were unable to figure out the negative reaction.

On the other hand, Judy was delighted that her father remarried. She was glad her father had something to live for again, and, in addition, she was relieved of the burden of worrying about him and caring for him.

In an attempt to figure out why adult children react as they do to their parents' retirement, remarriage, and possible move, I interviewed a group of them. One daughter, age 30, was dismayed when her parents retired and moved to California. She said, "I have heard of children leaving home, but not parents leaving home! What's going on?" Another son felt betrayed that his parents had "deserted" their grandchildren.

Many children expressed concern that their parents would have time on their hands or perhaps become depressed. Others worried about the cost of healthcare eating up their parents' income and savings. Some felt rejected by their parents' involvement with retirement activities. A comedy sketch from an original Florida Studio Theatre production of "Laughing Matters" illustrated this point. An adult woman called her retired mother saying she needed her mother's advice. However, her mother was booked up with meetings, golf games, hair appointment, bridge lessons, and so forth. Dejected, the daughter hung up the phone. She then saw an ad for an 800 number, "Dial a Mom." She immediately called and heard the following: "This is your substitute Mom. Press 1 if you want a sympathetic mom; press 2 for a critical mom; press 3 if you want a mom to discuss money; press 4 if you want your mom to baby-sit."

There are many retired couples who move to be near their adult children and grandchildren. For some adult children, it is a relief to have extra help and support; for others it feels like a responsibility to be sure they see enough of their retired parents. Especially in cases where one of the parents dies, the tendency is to rely heavily on the adult children, whose lives are already complicated with work and raising children. Unresolved issues can crop up between adult children and their parents—issues that were on the back burner when everyone was busy working. Again, there is no simple solution.

One woman suggested an "expectation exchange" meeting, where the parents and children expressed what they expected of the relationship now that the retired parents had moved to be closer to the grandchildren. She said it was awkward at first, but eventually the meeting cleared the air. The retired parents had expected a regular Friday night dinner together with the family. But the parents were too busy, too absorbed in their own social life and their children's activities. They decided to "play it by ear" but revisit the issue from time to time.

You might try your own version of an "expectation exchange." Clearing the air is the best strategy. It can work in many instances. However, in cases of extreme anger or jealousy, professional counseling may be needed.

Caretaking: Giving Back or Being Trapped?

Now that people are living longer, the possibilities increase that caretaking will be part of the retirement years, whether it be caretaking for a spouse, an adult child, a grandchild, a parent, or another relative. This new pattern is one for which we have no road maps.

Little did Yolanda suspect that her life would be consumed with caretaking when she remarried. Because her husband was older and retired, she too retired from her teaching job. She started making and selling jewelry. Then, her mother broke her hip and needed constant care. Today, after 10 years, Yolanda is still involved with her mother. How does she cope with such a burden over such a long period? She credits her faith, her church attendance, and participation in a support group as her saving grace.

Another couple retired to Arizona for fun, golf, and flying their own airplane. Soon after their retirement their daughter was diagnosed with a life-threatening disease. They had no conflict about what to do—bring her to live with them. She is now, after 10 years, almost totally disabled. Their lives revolve around caretaking. They maintain a social life, including golf and cards, but clearly their life is not what it had been, nor what they had expected it to be.

Then, too, I interviewed Mel, a retired mail carrier for the postal service. His plan had been to retire to Pennsylvania, where he had several nieces and an aunt. Just as he was preparing to retire, his adult daughter received a five-year prison sentence on a narcotics charge. Mel stepped in, assuming full-time responsibility for his baby granddaughter. In fact, he brought his grandchild to the interview.

Mel was fearful about the future. What would happen when his daughter was released from prison? Mel had little confidence in her because she had been on and off drugs since age 10. Although totally committed to his granddaughter, Mel admits to feeling he has been cheated out of his retirement years.

More than three million families are involved in grandparents raising grandchildren.[9] This growing problem has spawned a number of programs offering support to those grandparents. As one example, the University of Maryland, with funding from the National Institute of Mental Health, identified grandparents and trained them to go into their own communities and establish support groups for other grandparents. On the national level, advocacy groups began pushing for legislation to provide benefits for custodial grandparents.

The issue of caretaking—whether it is for a spouse, a friend, a parent, or a grandchild—affects almost everyone at some time. Marcia's life fell apart when she was trapped taking care of her husband and granddaughter. She found a support group that dealt with issues such as, "What is the meaning of life," "How to keep our spirits up when those around us are ill." They shared feelings of resentment, anger, and guilt. Erma Bombeck's statement, "Guilt is the gift that keeps on giving," became their mantra. Caregivers need to engage in self-care, using every source of support. Seeking out support groups can help control guilt, set limits, and build in time for enjoyment.

Suddenly Alone

For those who shared most of their lives with a partner, widowhood or divorce means a wrenching adjustment. Retirement can complicate matters, as there is no job to provide a few hours of respite. Reactions to loss of a partner vary a great deal. Madeline talked about how much she wanted her husband back, but because that was impossible, she confessed that she would give anything to have a man in her life again. Liz painted a contrasting picture, when she stated emphatically, "I will never live with anyone again. Finally, I can come and go as I please, even read in the middle of the night."

For those who move to another community during retirement, and then become widowed, the question is whether to stay. The greatest pull is to move nearer their adult children. For Marcy, whose son and daughter-in-law urged her to move near them, it worked out well. Six months after the move, Marcy reported that she was happy. In addition to being with her family, she had joined two bridge groups and enrolled in two noncredit courses at the local university.

The flip side: Adult children and grandchildren have their own lives. With the best of intentions, adult children invite you to be near them, but often the time they spend with you does not meet your expectations.

Even if you are in a community where you are known, where you have friends, where once you and your spouse had a satisfying social life with other couples, you will have to face big adjustments.

If you are lucky, your group will continue including you in whatever they do. However, many others echoed Sally's story. She reported, "Suddenly it was, 'Let's have lunch,' or 'The girls are going to the discount mall. Want to come?' But about weekends— especially Saturday nights—there never was a word. What a letdown."

We cannot forget those of you who live alone by choice. Retirement is an adjustment, but the one thing that is stable is the fact that you do not have to adjust to a changed relationship pattern. But you, like others, still have decisions to make about where to live and how to forge a meaningful lifestyle.

For those who have no family, the key to a successful retirement is friendship.

"MAKE NEW FRIENDS BUT KEEP THE OLD—
ONE IS SILVER, THE OTHER GOLD"

As we previously discussed, it is clear that a major disadvantage of retirement is losing contact with co-workers. Friends outside of work become increasingly important, often substituting for colleagues.

To uncover how retirement alters participants' friendships, Nancy Pinson-Milburn, Penny Hartman, and George Milburn conducted a focus group with retirees in Frederick, Maryland.[10] One woman commented, "I moved away from family to California. Now friends are my family." Another woman claimed, "I am now majoring in social life—we are out every day either for lunch or dinner with friends. I never had time for that before." Women reported a variety of changes in both the quantity and quality of their friendships. After retirement, they moved from a smaller circle of friends to a larger group of acquaintances. Many found their local senior center, with its large variety of activities, a wonderful place to congregate.

There are many ways that retired people can make new friends. For example, travel is big business, and many retirees participate in cruises, driving vacations, tours, and Elderhostels. In fact, almost 200,000 individuals went on Elderhostel trips in 1999.[11] Others are using the Internet to make new acquaintances. An article in a *New York Times* special section on retirement called "Finding a Substitute for Office

Chitchat" told about a retiree who "realized that I was a very social animal. . . . After you walk the dog, what do you do?"[12] He eventually found out about the Third Age Web site, designed for those in late middle age.

Many retirees meet and make new friends by participating in educational activities. In most areas, there are universities that offer courses to seniors. In Sarasota, Florida, there are at least six separate organizations offering courses for retirees. Some are freestanding, others part of a university, and some sponsored by Elderhostel.

In a focus group I conducted with Barbara Jacobs the participants reported the ease with which they all become friends after moving south.[13] They met while dancing at senior centers three to four afternoons each week, claiming that you are never too old to make significant connections. I asked them what advice they would give to the person who said "retirement is hollow." They answered, "Get a life! Get out, dance, meet people, go on trips, and take courses. Anything but sit at home."

On the other side, Natalie and Maury are not seeking out new friendships. They say they will never leave their hometown in the Midwest because the ties with close friends are so strong, the roots so deep, that moving would be out of the question. Curiously, none of the couple's three children or grandchildren live nearby.

The value of friendship, especially to women, is critical to well-being. In a landmark study, a number of researchers found that the more friends women had, the longer they lived and stayed in better health. Advice: Do not put making and nurturing friendships on the back burner. They will provide you with joy, companionship, and support. Friendship is one of the best buffers to stress and can make the difference in a happy retirement.[14]

The Downside: Being Left Out

Friendship, critical as it is, has a potential downside. Friendships after retirement have the same problems as at any other time of life—sometimes it takes work to get along together, feel accepted, and find mutual enjoyment. However, because friendships can loom especially important during retirement, when things do not go well the issues are painful, often reminiscent of adolescence.

One couple, for example, went on a cruise with others from the community in which they lived. They felt left out, because those they considered the "top clique" did not invite them to join their table for dinner. To the naked eye, the trip appeared to be wonderful. But when interviewing the travelers after the trip, I found it had been wonderful only for the "top group."

Along a similar line, Sylvia's father felt "marginalized" at the upscale retirement center in which he lived. He had been a shoe salesman. Sylvia, however, became a lawyer and married the CEO of a large company. When her father retired because of failing health, she was able to finance his move into an upscale retirement and assisted-living complex near her. They both expected it to provide numerous activities and friends. However, he felt left out. When other residents asked him what he had done before, he replied "feet." The residents assumed he was a physician specializing in feet. When he clarified, saying he had been a shoe salesman, they lost interest. Among this group of retirees, obviously, past status determined friendships.

It is important to stop investing time and energy in people who, for whatever reason, are not open to being your friend. Phyllis retired and moved to a town in the West where her best friend lived. This best friend introduced her to all of her friends and included her in their book club. When she tried to strike up friendships with several women in the club, she was rejected. She even was "shunned" by one of the members when they bumped into each other at social functions. Phyllis began to wonder what was wrong with herself. With help, she began to reframe. She decided to drop out of the book club and not spend time with people who made her feel diminished. Instead, she became involved in a lifelong learning project and other community groups. She then began to make friends who had similar interests. The process took almost two years.

Phyllis said, "It is freeing when you realize that you don't have to take 'guff' from people. I feel much better now that I have forged out on my own. I am not going to be in situations where I get negative feedback."

LOCATION, LOCATION, LOCATION

We have discussed an approach to healthy living in these last two chapters—taking care of your body, mental health, soul, finances, and relationships. But where you live is part of the picture. Is your environment user-friendly? Is it a healthy environment that makes you feel comfortable and good about yourself?

Increasingly, magazines, books, and even Web sites provide information about how much money you need in retirement and how to find the right place to live. These two issues—money and location—are intertwined.

Maria, a seamstress, moved to the United States from Mexico. She had some health problems—knee and eye—but could not afford medical care until turning 65, when she became eligible for Medicare. However, the delay had caused problems that forced her to retire.

In some ways she likes being retired, but she finds that she is barely able to make ends meet on Social Security and the small jobs she can manage to do. Maria's quandary: Where should she live? If she stays in the United States, she continues to receive Social Security and Medicare. On the other hand, she owns a small apartment in Mexico that is near family.

Maria's dilemma of where to live, whether to move, and how to spend her remaining years is a question faced by many contemplating retirement. Our image of retirees moving to sunny Florida or California is true for some. But according to one survey, 83% of the respondents prefer retiring near their homes. TIAA-CREF, the largest insurance company handling annuities for teachers, found that although many move after retirement, only 28% move to another part of the country.[15] Of those who move, most relocate close to their former homes.

According to sociologist Charles F. Longino, retirement migration from the Northeast and Midwest to Florida, and from Western states to California, Arizona, and Texas, has plateaued.[16] However, other states—North Carolina, Washington, Virginia, and Georgia—are now attracting more retirees than they once did.

We all probably know people who moved to a retirement community, only to return to their original hometown—usually where an adult child is living, often because of failing health or the death of a spouse. I, therefore, asked Professor Longino about the numbers who return to their original homes. He wrote that there is "[n]o way to tell with census data. There are 'counter-streams' going from the more common destination states (in opposite direction from the larger flow—e.g., Florida to New York). . . . The characteristics of people in the counter-streams, however, are older, more often widowed, more often returning to a state in which they were born. All of this supports the hypothesis that there may be a fairly high proportion of people returning home in the counter-stream. But there is no way of actually knowing."[17]

Aside from moving to another state, another option is the movement started by women to band together, share housing, and continue working, writing, and creating. The need is tremendous. Between 1970 and 1998, "the number of women living alone . . . doubled, from 7.3 million to 15.3 million. . . . In New York City . . . 41.8% of all women age 65 and older live alone, versus 20.8% of the men. To help alleviate loneliness, the National Shared House Resource Center helps match women with appropriate facilities."[18]

Once a location has been decided, along comes another choice: your housing. There are so many options: moving to a condo, co-op, mobile home, single family unit, tree house, or retirement villages. Longino reported that only about 10% of retired persons are living in retirement communities. Also, boomers do not find the prospect of a retirement community appealing, according to a report in *The Wall Street Journal*.[19]

A woman in her 90s, who still dances competitively, was urged to move into the retirement complex where her 70-year-old son and daughter-in-law live. She does not feel ready yet! On the other hand, many find the community spirit in retirement villages very rewarding. As with all kinds of living, it is important to test the waters and really explore where you are going to land.

Recently I received a letter describing a friend's experience when she moved into a condo. "My husband had just been elected president of the condo association (and I was jokingly referred to as First Lady) when our son came to visit. As we walked to the elevator, a woman looked at me, and before I could introduce my son to her, she turned on her heels and walked briskly away. As we walked down to the pool, I approached two men, who mildly acknowledged my hello and turned their backs. My son asked what had happened. I explained that the problem related to a decision made by the board to eliminate pets in the building. Clearly, pet owners—a minority—were outraged. So in a period of two weeks I went from 'First Lady' to 'First Pariah.' "

The details and content of the dispute are irrelevant. What is this really all about? The underlying issues are understandable. Many residents in any institutional facility give up some control. One example relates to pets. In your own home you can decide whether or not to have a dog and or cat. Most condos and apartments have pet rules. Some prohibit pets; others allow pets of a certain size. Despite the need for rules, many find an upside to moving into a condo or retirement community. As one person reported, "It is wonderful not to have snow removal problems or pool cleaning."

During the course of my interviewing, I visited some mobile home parks. Most of the residents I spoke with were very enthusiastic about their living situation.

For the most part, their enjoyment of this living arrangement resulted from seeing this as a positive move. Many of the couples were blue-collar workers and never expected to be able to afford a second home. For them, this was a "step up" in the world. The freedom to "go to the mall with the girls," "go fishing with the guys," and dance at the senior center, seemed like "heaven."

When Laura's husband died, she took over the family business. After she raised her three children, she sold the business and her large home, and moved to an urban area. She now lives in a 600-square-foot apartment. On the surface, moving from a 4,000-square-foot house to a 600-square-foot apartment looks like a "step down." But not to her. She loves living in a small space, entertains by taking people out, and wouldn't change her situation for anything.

Laura's appraisal consisted of two parts: (1) She saw the move as positive and under her control and (2) she saw her resources as plentiful. She had emotional and financial support and was thrilled with her new lifestyle. At the risk of oversimplifying, how one evaluates a 600- or 4,000-square-foot space is in the "eye of the beholder."

When choosing a location or living situation, the issue to consider is whether the arrangement is a healthy one that will prevent illness and promote wellness, and whether the relationships you will have there are meaningful and supportive. There is no magic living arrangement; each has its plusses and minuses.

No one can answer these questions for you better than you can answer them for yourself. But, as gigantic a decision as moving may be, remember: As in all things during retirement, nothing needs to be forever. Whatever decision you make, it is important to keep in mind all the options. They are part of the wonderful choices you have in finding your retirement path.

If you've always wanted to try a new place or new climate, a new lifestyle, and you want to adventure, give it a go. Many experiment. They rent in a new place before selling their old home and moving. If you want to continue with life as it has been, stay put. Remember, the road goes two ways: You can always return if it does not work out. In the end, you rarely regret the things you've done in life—you regret those you didn't.

TRANSITION TIPS

☞ **Tip 1. Build up your social equity**. Most people spend hours figuring out how much money they will have during retirement. Equally important is figuring how you will replace your feelings of belonging and status. Look for new friends to replace work relationships.

☞ **Tip 2. Once again, patience is required**. For those who live with a spouse or partner, retirement changes their interactions. Whose space is being invaded? Or is this a time for fun and rediscovering the reasons you originally got together? Working out these changes takes time, patience, empathy, understanding, and love.

☞ **Tip 3. Explore living options carefully.** There are many possible living arrangements. Trial vacations designed to test out different living locations and arrangements can be very helpful. What would it be like to move to a new community with few friends? How would you make friends? What have others experienced? Answers to these and other questions can help with your decision making.

☞ **Tip 4. Initiate an Expectation Exchange with partners, parents, or adult children.** One woman became upset with her adult children for not calling enough whereas another man continually felt guilty that he was unable to visit his mother in her retirement home as much as she wanted. It is often helpful to engage the services of a social worker, counselor, or psychologist to meet with both generations. These meetings would enable all parties to freely express what each expected and then resolve what each could do. To assist you in assessing your social equity, you may want to perform the following *Relationship Audit*.

Your Relationship Audit

Compare your relationships pre-retirement and now by filling in the two circles—first "My Pre-Retirement Circle of Friends and Acquaintances" and then "My Current Circle of Friends and Acquaintances." These graphic representations of your social relationships will show you how those relationships have changed as a result of retirement.

Remember from the chapter discussion: The small circle in the middle is you. The next circle is for those with whom you are most intimate, followed by your close friends and family. The outermost circle represents those with whom you relate because of a role you play at work or in the community. These acquaintances are the most likely to change as a result of retirement.

For those preparing for retirement, fill in the circle describing your current relationships on "My Pre-Retirement Circle of Friends and Acquaintances," and underline the relationships you think will change as a result of retirement.

What can you do with this information? Filling out these circles enables you to compare pre- and post-retirement relationships in a graphic way. These circles will illustrate how retirement will alter, or has altered, your relationships. For example, if you find fewer opportunities (or expect to have fewer opportunities) to interact with friends, if you have lost people with whom to "schmooze," this is the time to figure out ways to network, to fill in the gaps. Of course, if you have lost people in your inner circle—your intimates—replacing those is not easy and takes time.

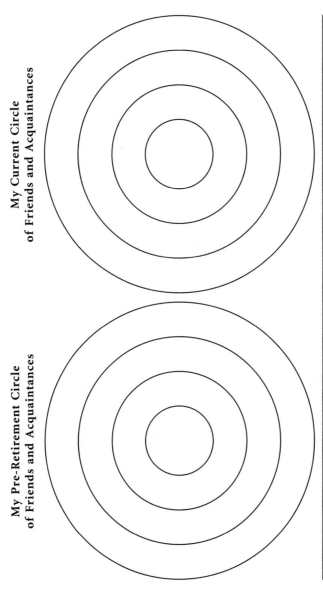

My Pre-Retirement Circle of Friends and Acquaintances

My Current Circle of Friends and Acquaintances

Note. From "Convoys Over the Life Course: Attachment, Roles, and Social Support," by R. L. Kahn and T. C. Antonucci, in *Life-Span Development and Behavior* (p. 273), by P. B. Baltes (Ed.), 1980, New York: Academic Press. Copyright 1980. Reprinted with permission from Elsevier.

4

Discovering Your Path

How do retirees restructure their lives? What path do they follow after their main work activity? Although leaving work can create a tremendous void, over time it is possible to find rewarding ways to meet that challenge. According to sociologists Moen and Fields, some discernible trends exist for those retired people they studied:

- Almost 39% of retired men and about 20% of retired women are working part time.
- 45% of the men and 62% of the women volunteer for more than 10 hours a week.
- 61% of the men and 51% of the women participate in community organizations.[1]

The work participation rates were higher for people who were newly retired; that is, over time, employment dropped off. According to Stan Hinden, former *Washington Post* reporter, these figures were confirmed by two major surveys that indicate that 80% of the 76 million people born between 1946 and 1964 plan to

work at least part time after retirement.[2] Survey participants said that they work partly because they need the
income, but also because they value the sense of worth
and structure work gives to their lives.

To test out the hypotheses that retirees want to
work, the Economic Development Council of the Bra-
denton, Florida, Chamber of Commerce conducted
focus groups.[3] Although the study was limited to one
geographical area, the results seem generally applicable—that most retirees wanted to work part time in
paid activities, but with certain conditions. They
wanted flexible hours and opportunities to travel and
visit family, especially grandchildren. Even though
most employers are normally unable to accommodate
these wishes, when there is a tight labor market, employers will work out special conditions.

In addition to paid work, volunteering has become
big business. Many retirees reported that it "was time
to give back." Others volunteered because there were
no paid opportunities. In both instances, "recognition"
was important.

During the course of my research on retirement,
it became clear that people take markedly different
paths as they structure their lives to obtain the recognition, satisfaction, and meaning they received through
work. Most of the retirees took one of the following
paths as they proceeded with the task of getting a
new life:

- *Continuers* for whom identity in previous work,
  home, or volunteer life is still central;

- *Adventurers* who have moved in new directions, whether paid or unpaid;
- *Searchers* who are separating from the past but who have not yet found their place;
- *Easy Gliders* who are content, enjoy retirement, go with the flow; and
- *Retreaters* who have given up on forging a new, rewarding life.

These are general categories, and retirees may fall into more than one. Also, from time to time, retirees shift from one category into another. As stated previously, we need to begin thinking of retirement not as a finite experience but as a process in which a retirement career evolves just as a work career did. You can read on to help determine whether the path you are on is the most fulfilling one for you.

CONTINUERS:
MORE OF THE SAME, BUT DIFFERENT

Continuers package their principal activities in new ways. They stay connected with their past skills, activities, interests, and values, but modify them to fit retirement. Although some important aspects of their life have changed, they continue to maintain their identification with, and commitment to, their previous work, either through part-time paid work or volunteer activities.

Gil is an example of a Continuer. The developer of a leading paper company, he sold his business for an enormous profit. After a six-month, around-the-world trip with his wife, they decided that retirement was not for them. They loved the paper business but wanted to do something different. They started a small shop selling handmade papers with an attached workshop where people could learn how to make their own paper gifts. They continued certain aspects of their previous life by being in business around paper, but they were continuing in new ways.

Margaret, another Continuer, was formerly the vice president of an educational technology center. As a way to ease her retirement transition, she made a conscious decision to shift from full-time to part-time work within the same organization. During the year before retiring, she moved her activities from the office to her home. She developed new connections, but all within her field of computers and technology. She started a business with a colleague, continued working a limited number of hours at her previous job, and joined the board of a national professional organization. Now she teaches part time and does some corporate consulting. Meanwhile, she is overseeing construction of a gazebo by her pool, where she will set up an outside office. The content of what she does is a modification of what she did before. "At this stage I find myself weaving together predominant threads of my past career: teaching, technology, and career development."

ADVENTURERS: SOMETHING NEW

Adventurers see retirement as an opportunity to start new endeavors, new ways of organizing their personal time and space. To be classified as an Adventurer, it is necessary to develop and exercise new skills, new energies.

For 10 years I've been part of a luncheon group with three other women. We call ourselves "The Committee of Four." We have such fun, such interesting conversations, and such meaningful interchanges that we make these lunches a high priority. After several years, we began an annual dinner that included husbands.

As we were toasting each other at one of these dinners, we realized that all of the toasts related to new ventures we were undertaking. Each couple was moving on, changing course, and creating options. A retired professor and a former government employee who is, in general, a mover and a shaker, had begun their new chapter by marrying. A lecturer at a university and her husband, a government official, had just left their jobs to spend a year traveling around the world, learning to play the piano, and doing whatever else caught their fancy.

A former law professor and practicing lawyer and his wife, a therapist, were also making a major change: They had recently moved from their family house to an apartment and bought a small second home on the coast in California. And my husband Steve and I were selling our apartment and moving to another city to build a new life in a new venue.

We were all creating new structures for our lives, experimenting with new ways to relate to work, love, and play. As stated in the introduction, it is this potential that makes this time in life—for those who are in good health, with adequate income—a time of challenge, a moving toward instead of a moving from. At that moment, we were all Adventurers.

There are lots of ways to be an Adventurer. For some retirees, adventuring means leaving one type of paid work for another. Take the example of Bob, who ran an environmental research program for the U.S. Congress. When funding for his program was terminated, he had a year on salary to think about what to do next. He opted for working, standard Washington style, as a consultant. But after two years he acknowledged that this activity was not rewarding, and he needed a change.

An enthusiastic sailor, he took a sailing trip to consider his future. His first idea—becoming a sailing instructor—seemed too hedonistic. Then Bob remembered how he had emerged from a traumatic time earlier in his life, when his wife had died, his young son was in turmoil, and Bob had developed a terrible back problem. He went to many specialists, none of whom helped. Finally he went to a massage therapist. To his amazement, the therapist relieved his back problem.

The more Bob thought about defining moments in his life, the more he realized he wanted to help people as he had been helped—by becoming a massage therapist. His new wife was supportive, but many of his friends—especially men—were shocked. To them, the choice was incongruous with the Bob they had known as a briefcase-toting, serious professional. When Bob enrolled in massage school, he found an interesting group of former lawyers, doctors, young people, and retirees. The program was intense, requiring 1,000 hours of training. When he became a practicing massage therapist, he felt focused and very proud. He loves receiving immediate feedback from clients, the flexibility of his schedule, and the challenge of succeeding as an entrepreneur.

Bob's identity as an Adventurer emerged after he was forced into involuntary retirement. He actually feels lucky that he is not a rich man and was forced to develop an alternative that would allow him to earn some retirement income.

Seth provides another example of an Adventurer. Starting at age 10, he worked in a pharmacy until he retired at age 70. Every day he had a place to go, a structure for his time. On his first day after retirement he told his wife, "I don't know what to do, where to go. How will I spend my days?" For several months Seth mostly moped around the house. Then one day his son, recalling that his dad had enjoyed baseball when he was younger, suggested that his father try out for the senior league. Uncertain whether he wanted to, Seth nevertheless tried out, made the team, and for more than two years his life has been restructured positively.

His former routine of working from 6 a.m. until 7 p.m. has been replaced with a seasonal baseball schedule, structured around practice and games. He has changed his role from that of general manager of a small business to that of baseball player. His relationships have also changed. Now, instead of relating primarily to business acquaintances, he has developed a rewarding fellowship with other retirees in the league. Even his assumptions about himself and his life have changed. He has equal or more status than before, is having a good time, and is at peace with the world.

Joy suggests another model of Adventurer—one who transformed herself from a high-powered business executive to a productive volunteer in new fields. At a national magazine, she wrote market appraisals and formulated sales promotion plans for 40 major U.S. markets. Her other top corporate jobs had been in sales, special events, and publicity.

Almost immediately after retiring she moved to a new community, one where she had family. Joy took on leadership roles in her new community. She became involved in groups as diverse as the arts council and an experimental college. In each case, the former executive initiated new activities and brought schools, community, and the arts into close communication. As a former president of a woman's group, she initiated programs that have reached women of all ages and economic levels in the community.

Applying the same vigor to her retirement that she applied to her career in business, Joy has really turned into the model Adventurer retiree. With three other retired women, she speaks before groups, offering advice on how to make the most of retirement. To her, retirement is like everything else: "You mobilize your resources and move on." As both Bob, Seth, and Joy have found, new adventures can be invigorating.

Searchers: Looking for Your Niche

Because retirement is a time of exploring new options for life structure and activities, it is a path marked by trial and error. It is not unusual for a retiree to start on one path, find that it is not satisfying, and to resume searching. Most of us probably fall into this category at one or more times during our retirement.

Cheryl retired from her job at a federal government agency two years ago. She has no regrets and does not miss her work. But for the entire two years she has been searching. She told me the following:

> I still have not found my niche. I flit from thing to thing. I tried local politics and it was fun, but after the election there was nothing for me. I volunteered to work at the White House, but after six weeks realized I would forever be licking envelopes. I do mediation one day a week, but need something else to challenge me. I feel as if I am just moving from one organization to another.

Betty, an administrative assistant to a trade organization, had no conflict about retiring. For her, it meant time to finally play. Although she had worked off and on in paying jobs, she considered her main activity being a mother and wife, and said she experienced "vicarious pleasure" from her husband's career. However, three years after her retirement, Betty began to question the absence of focus. She felt that her life was "without value, useless." She realized that when people at parties asked her what she did, and she responded, "I'm playing," the questioner seemed to lose interest in her.

After considering many options, Betty decided to become a docent at an art gallery. She applied and was turned down by several museums in Minneapolis. She became so discouraged that she wouldn't even ask why she was not accepted. However, she decided to try once more. When she was accepted, her two-year search for something useful to do had finally ended. She had stuck with Plan A—becoming a docent—because she had not yet figured out a Plan B!

Betty's search required dealing with rejection—a not uncommon experience. It reminds me of my own search. My original goal was to secure a special title and relationship with a local university; then I tried for a connection with a major businesswoman. Neither of these worked out. My Plan B was writing this book, something I would have skipped over if my Plan A had been successful.

Milton, a dentist, has seemingly been implementing his Plans, A, B, C, D, and E, all at the same time. An expert on reconstructive surgery and an esteemed member of a medical school faculty, Milton began his retirement process by phasing down to part-time work and then gradually leaving the faculty entirely. Now, five years after retirement, Milton is in what he describes as a period of "exploration." He has many tutors—a piano tutor, an exercise trainer, and a computer expert. When I asked if learning to play the piano was the realization of a former dream, he emphatically said, "No." It's simply one phase of his explorations. In addition to his learning activities, Milton is enjoying new friends he has met at a health club, his grandchildren, and a very active travel schedule. By moving slowly, over a period of five years, he had made time to attend to feelings engendered by exiting his life role. He used this period for experimentation and exploration, rather than committing himself to a determined plan of action. Milton, in fact, could turn out to be a full-time, permanent Searcher, who, by the way, loves every minute of the process.

Lois retired six years ago. She did not miss a beat. She knew exactly what she wanted to do: expand her involvement in the League of Women Voters. After two years she became president of the local group. This engaged her totally. However, she is now, for the first time, becoming a Searcher. Her presidency is at an end, and she is studying what everyone is doing in retirement, trying to figure out her next engagement.

Exploring lifestyles and experimenting with new interests leads to some wild goose chases, but it can end up with main gains. This is similar to the trials and errors of many high school and college graduates as they try to figure out what's next.

Easy Gliders: Content To Go With the Flow

Another category of retirees enjoy unscheduled time, select activities that appeal to them, and pace themselves according to their newfound freedom. They want to relax and embrace the retirement ride—sometimes meandering, sometimes working, and sometimes involved with family and friends. I asked several people what term to use for this category. They suggested: Easy Glider, Easy Rider, Free Player, Pacer, and Meanderer. Several liked free player. One woman wrote, "Free Player connotes people who swing with the culture . . . not bound by what one group might think . . . ready to try something new if it appeals, and if it doesn't, so what?" One man said, "I love Riders. These are the folks who go along for the ride. . . . They have earned the ride." And another man, still working, wrote, "I like the idea of Meanderer. That has a relaxed, free-spirit ring to it, and I think if I ever retire, you've found my niche with Meanderer." Despite the excellent advice, I selected Easy Gliders.

My editor, Esther Gordon, said she does not fit into the categories of Continuer, Adventurer, Searcher, or

Retreater. Although she still works part time, the aspect of retirement she likes best is unscheduled time. She wrote, "In the back of my mind I want serendipity . . . to spend some time indulging in things that give me pleasure, and making others (especially my grandchildren) happy. I've completed Plan A. I do not want a Plan B. I just want to be!" Esther, an aficionado of Latin jazz, has begun bongo lessons. To her choice of lifestyle she says "Olé!"

Similarly, Jean, a mover and a shaker who hosted a television public affairs show and served on the school board, faced a serious illness and came through it. She reevaluated her life and is now enjoying an early retirement. She enjoys each day—kayaking, swimming, and entertaining; taking time for fun, friends, and family, and for responsibilities and community involvement. She is open to new experiences but is neither searching nor continuing with what she did. She is free-wheeling.

Then there is Mike who worked hard all his life. He now wants to relax and enjoy the retirement ride. He started working when he was 16 and feels he is entitled to enjoy friends, family, daily exercise, and time to loaf. His wife is always telling him to get busy, do something "constructive." Been there, done that, he replies. He is not a Retreater, neither does he want to continue what he did, or search for something new. He too is a Glider.

Easy Gliders are open to anything, but are still in control. They are eclectic and have qualities of all the other types—occasionally adventuring, searching, continuing and retreating, just enough to catch their breath.

RETREATERS: GIVING UP

Sometimes it can be difficult to tell whether Retreaters are just taking time out—a moratorium from life—or whether they are disengaging from life entirely. David is an example of the latter.

Forced by poor eyesight to retire from his job editing a scientific journal, David had a lot of time on his hands. "I had always expected to see my old friends, do information projects, use my expertise after retirement." But after a while, his former network was no longer there.

David had worked for the same employer for 44 years. He was unaccustomed to change, and admitted that he did not have the "resiliency or skill to handle this kind of crisis." He made some efforts toward building a new life. Failing to get part-time work, he developed a project for the Smithsonian Institution, but it faltered when money ran out. Working as a museum volunteer, the only man in his area, he reported, "I experienced sexism. The women in the office always went to lunch but never once invited me to join them." With his eye problems getting worse, David said, "I engage in no activities. I gave up driving four years ago. I am a guy who is not very resourceful."

He seemed resigned to his current state of retreat. However, we will see in the next chapter the combination of forces that pushed him out of the Retreater path.

A COMBINATION PATH

Malcolm, formerly a survey and market researcher for AT&T, retired at age 65. He and his wife stayed in their hometown where he continued his research activities as an independent consultant. He developed a two-day training program in the use of focus groups, taught courses for Elderhostel (one of which was "Polls, Pollsters, and Poll Cats") and ran focus groups for the Chamber of Commerce. He was continuing to do work that he formerly did, but this time for himself.

But Malcolm yearned for something new and more creative in retirement. Intrigued by its title, he signed up for a course on "Magic as Therapy." This unleashed a new endeavor. He used magic as a vehicle for reaching out to people in nursing homes. Feeling invigorated at 70, Malcolm combines two paths: continuing his work from the past, but adventuring into new areas. He has a new hobby, too: building model ships. And who knows where he will be in five years?

Whenever I present the five categories, people immediately jump to identify themselves. Many report that they are combinations. As one recently retired professor said, "I am an Adventurer from taking up genealogy, a Continuer because I am still writing in my field, and a Searcher because I have not yet identified my focus." Another man about to retire from medicine, said, "I know what I am going to do—consult and teach. I will be a Continuer for a while and then become a Searcher to find new activities and new ventures."

Many baby boomers contemplating retirement are beginning to think of new paths to follow. One woman, a respected judge and still at the height of her career, has an engrossing hobby—collecting gems and making jewelry. Her plan is to take this up in a focused way after retirement. In the meantime, she is working and building for her future.

How Does Identifying Your Path Help?

Retirement used to mean giving up work. Now there are many retirement models—retiring from one career or job and replacing it with another; continuing in paid work, earning income on a part-time basis; working on a regular schedule as a volunteer; going back to school; or simply "playing," luxuriating in having enough time to devote to family and social life, or tennis or music or magic or any other personal interest. Instead of the traditional pattern of education, work, and retirement, the lines have blurred to the point where all three of these life activities may take place at the same time, or even alternatively.

How does identifying your pattern help? In my case, I realized I was clearly a Continuer. I wanted to retire, but I am not interested in sports, taking new courses, or developing new skills. Once I recognized that, I had to figure how to continue with some of the things that had made me feel useful before. I therefore volunteered for an organization serving the same kind of population with whom I had worked previously. I also began consulting with other organizations that used some of the skills I had used in my work as a professor. In other words, I am a combination. Mostly a Continuer, I adventured by moving into a new community and trying to make new friends while keeping the old. The truth seems to be that we are all combinations, albeit with a dominant one. The combination will continually change throughout life.

On the other hand, Phyllis realized that she was a kind of Continuer, but not a Continuer of her work activities. She wanted to continue with leisure activities that she had loved as a college student—tennis, walking, and sports. She searched for ways to make that happen.

Then there was Bob, an Adventurer. He knew he wanted something new after leaving the government. As we saw, he adventured into new, uncharted territory. Larry also realized he wanted something new after spending 25 years on the assembly line. After a period of searching, he adventured into new waters, dancing at least four times a week. He compared himself favorably to his friend, Will, who left the line and retreated to his couch, watching television and drinking beer.

And Mary, who worked all her life, is just enjoying each day as it comes. However, she knows that someday she will want something more. She will search and hopefully find a path that suits her when she is ready.

The act of retiring from a job or a career sets off ripples that extend into our personal, daily, and emotional life, raising issues of identity, of not feeling appreciated, of belonging to a community and engaging in meaningful activities. Exiting successfully from one life into a new one takes energy and often a great deal of time. But as we have seen, there are many fruitful ways to approach this challenge: as a Continuer, Adventurer, Easy Glider, or Searcher. I hope none of us will settle for being a Retreater because, as we have seen from the stories in this chapter, although there is no single, magic path to satisfaction, there are many options from which to create a successful life.

TRANSITION TIPS

☞ **Tip 1. Start a group, "What's Next?"** At a recent meeting of a group designed to discuss "What's Next?" the members decided to focus on what paths they were taking. One woman said, "I was a professor. After retirement, we moved to another state to be closer to our grandchildren. I expected to be a Continuer but found no outlets for teaching in my field. So now I am a Searcher, but not a happy one." The group brainstormed ways she could still be a Continuer. One member of the group connected her with a local university that housed a program where retirees taught other retirees. She is now teaching and meeting lots of others in her same situation. Group discussions regarding your path can be a great help in clarifying what you want and brainstorming ways to make your goal a reality.

☞ **Tip 2. Know your path**. With all these options, how can anyone even begin to figure out what path to take? To identify your path, fill out the questionnaire on the next page, "Which Retirement Path Is Yours?" This will be a start. You can figure out if that is the path you want and, if not, what to do about it.

WHICH RETIREMENT PATH IS YOURS?

Take this simple quiz to determine which category best matches you. Circle the letter that best matches your choice.

1. *Do you usually*
   a. Enjoy traveling to new places?
   b. Seek out friends wherever you go?
   c. Stick to the same group you've been in for years?
   d. Take each day as it comes?
   e. Prefer to be alone?

2. *For leisure time, do you usually*
   a. Seek out new and challenging activities?
   b. Try an activity, and if it doesn't suit you, drop it and try something else?
   c. Continue the same hobbies you've always had?
   d. Finally take the time to "smell the roses"?
   e. Not have hobbies or outside interests?

3. *Is your current job or activity*
   a. Very different from anything you have ever done before?
   b. Prompting you to look elsewhere for more challenges?
   c. The enjoyable, satisfying way in which you spend your time?
   d. Enjoyable, but without urgency and concern with the end result?
   e. Overwhelming?

4. *If a project doesn't work out, do you usually*

    a. Begin something new?

    b. Not mind; you will explore other options?

    c. Try again, but in the same, or allied, field?

    d. Take a deep breath and relax?

    e. Give up and look no further?

Scoring Instructions

Three or more A's mean you are an Adventurer; three or more B's mean you are a Searcher; three or more C's mean you are a Continuer; three or more D's mean you are an Easy Glider; and three or more E's mean you are a Retreater. Of course, you can be a combination. The following describes what your score means.

Adventurer

Adventurers see retirement as an opportunity to start new endeavors, to seek new challenges, and to organize personal time and space in new ways. Adventurers relish developing new skills. Their retirement path is different from their previous life.

Searcher

Searchers explore new paths, and move on until they find the one that suits them best. Searchers represent the largest group on the retirement scene. Exploring new options is a path marked by trial and error. It is not unusual for a retiree to start on one path, find that it is not satisfying, and resume searching for another. Few retirees are long-term or permanent Searchers, but most will fall into this category at one time or another.

Continuer

Continuers stay connected with their past skills, activities, interests, and values, but modify them to fit retirement. Work and work-related activities are very important, and Continuers try to maintain this identification through part-time paid or volunteer activities.

Easy Glider

Easy Gliders enjoy unscheduled time and select activities that appeal to them. They pace themselves according to their newfound freedom. They want to relax and embrace the retirement ride—sometimes meandering, sometimes working, sometimes involved with family, friends, and community activities. They are open to anything, yet are still in control. They are eclectic and have qualities of all the other types—occasionally adventuring, searching, continuing, and retreating.

Retreater

Retreaters are often difficult to spot. Sometimes the person is just taking time out—a needed moratorium—but other times, the person is disengaging from life. Retreaters find that time hangs heavy and that life is empty and depressing. Retreaters seem not to be very involved in or enthusiastic about any particular activities, and often avoid making new friends or acquaintances.

5

Taking Charge

As we have seen, each person experiences the transitions of retirement in a unique way. However, there is a structure that cuts across all transitions that can help you take charge. I will use Bob and David, already mentioned, as examples of how to take charge, and then show how my research-based framework can provide guidelines as you initiate or weather change.[1] The framework consists of three parts: *Understanding* your transitions, *Taking Stock* of your resources (the 4 S System), and *Taking Charge* by strengthening your resources.

UNDERSTANDING TRANSITIONS

What are other retirees doing? Sometimes it helps to know. We pick up ideas, and, most important, learn from their experiences. By keeping in touch with my former colleagues, I know they are still busily engaged in writing grants, teaching classes, and advising students. They probably wonder how I can be content to be away from the activities that constituted my daily routine for more than 40 years. Similarly, now that I've retired, I wonder how my former colleagues continue to be so totally engaged in work. It's because we live in different worlds. We have different *relationships* with our colleagues, different daily *routines*, different *roles*, and even different *assumptions* that affect both the structure of our lives and interactions not just with colleagues but with family, friends, and neighbors. And, as the new retiree soon finds out, replacing these relationships, routines, roles, and assumptions is an evolutionary process that occurs over time and often forces us to tolerate considerable uncertainty and even anxiety.

Remember Bob, described as an Adventurer who surprised his friends when he left his congressional research program to become a massage therapist? And David, described as a Retreater who found retirement underwhelming and depressing? They are prime examples that transitions do not happen at a specific hour, minute, or day. Transitions are a *process over time.* When Bob first left his job, he was extremely sad, almost depressed, because, he said, his "identity was fading away." He may have thought that simply by leaving his job he had made a transition. But the fact is that he had not completed the transition until the crucial aspects of the life that he had left behind had been replaced by something else.

Once again we are reminded that the process of developing new endeavors that engage our energy and commitment is time consuming and never ending. We saw this in chapter 4, when we discussed the different paths people might take and discovered that many were spending a great deal of time searching for the right niche.

Over time, as Bob filled the gaps in his life with a new set of *roles, relationships, routines,* and *assumptions,* he began to feel "absorbed, engaged, focused, and proud." But his journey had taken several paths: At first he was a Continuer, consulting in areas in which he had worked. He found this unsatisfactory. After a sailing trip during which he did much soul searching, he moved onto an Adventurer path. He became a massage therapist.

His training was intensive and difficult. He had periods of uncertainty. Was this an appropriate field for a man his age, he wondered? Would he make it? Although he was the oldest person in the class, he found a great deal of stimulation and stuck to it.

Another period of floundering followed his graduation. He was searching to establish a new work life. Over time, he developed a private practice, which he enjoyed, but then he began to feel isolated. When offered a part-time job at the massage school, he grabbed the opportunity. Finally, with the combination of private practice and work involvement, Bob felt fulfilled.

It has taken Bob several years to figure out his retirement path, which is understandable, taking into consideration how many facets of his life affected his retirement and, conversely, how retirement affected his life. And just when he thought he had everything in order, a new transition loomed. Doctors discovered that he had a slow-growing, rare, inoperable tumor. Shocked and distraught, he decided to take another sailing trip; perhaps it would be as helpful as his previous one for regaining inner equilibrium.

While at sea, Bob reminisced about his youth, spent in a town where, he recalled, the people looked grim and *were* grim. He concluded that, although he certainly had cause, he would not spend the rest of his life in that fashion.

Today, he is still working, determined to live fully and productively. He spends his leisure time working out and, in great measure, researching alternative treatments. He looks and still feels fine, except for minor symptoms.

David also experienced a major shift in his *role*, going from editing a scientific journal to having no role or mission. He lost many of his former work and professional *relationships*. His *routines* were gone, and he spent a great deal of time at home. Saddest of all, his *assumptions* changed: He began to see himself as a loser. His life was filled with many nonevents—mainly expectations about the way retirement would unfold.

It is interesting to note that we usually think of transitions as events—things that happened. But equally important are those events that you expect to happen but do not. David had expected to be a Continuer and to have others seek his wisdom. When he kept bumping up against dead ends, he began to realize that what he had expected was not occurring. Sometimes such nonevents can produce more sorrow because they are undercover.

Over several years, and several interviews, David's path evolved as he moved from Retreater to Continuer. In response to my questionnaire, he wrote,

> Declining vision had represented an alibi, absolving me from trying too hard. But it became a surprising asset! Because of my writing skills and sophistication in communications, I was invited to become a director of the Low Vision Information Center. I can feel useful without deluding myself. A spin-off: I wrote a detailed article on help for the low visioned for the national newsletter of another service organization concerned with seniors' health problems in general.
>
> In addition, I renewed a relationship with a very competent investigative reporter from my past. He supplied the entrepreneurial push that resulted in an article in TomPaine.com, an outlet for liberal journalism on the Internet . . .
>
> Tom Paine didn't make me a household word, but I sent my article to *The Washington Post* for possible reprint in the Outlook section. Out of the blue, the editor called saying he couldn't use this, but, since the presidential campaign was in process, would I compare the candidates' drug plans? I broadened the assignment . . . and offered a solution. Response was terrific, and I find myself embroiled in efforts to give this idea political wheels.
>
> In general, I would say retirement works best for those who have so many hobbies they don't need status, and those who have enough entrepreneurial skills to maintain a presence in the bigger world.

To sum up, from these examples we can see that what seems like a simple transition—retirement—is actually complicated. The process of taking charge of your retirement requires that you first understand the components of your transition. Bob's retirement involved multiple transitions, a change in his role, relationships, routines, and assumptions. His reactions changed over time. David's retirement was also connected with a health transition, and his experiences included many events and nonevents. You can look at your own retirement in the same way, assessing the degree to which retirement is connected to other transitions and the degree to which it changes your life. The more complex it is, the more it changes your life—for good or bad—and the more you will need to cope with it.

Now comes the $64,000 question: Even if I know all there is to know about a transition, how do I deal with it? That leads to our next section.

Taking Stock of Your Coping Resources: The 4 S System

Why do some of us breeze through what others may find a tragedy? Think back on the transitions in your life. You may find it puzzling that you pulled through one change smoothly only to flounder in the face of another. People react differently to different transitions because of their unique set of strengths and deficits.

The essence of the Transition Model is the categorization of potential resources so that people can make sense of why they are struggling or not struggling with a particular transition. Each person interviewed for this book approached retirement with different potential resources—*Situation*, *Self*, *Supports*, and *Strategies*. By taking stock of these resources, you can gain a picture of your own strengths and weaknesses.

Situation refers to the circumstances surrounding retirement. It involves answering questions such as the following: Are you free of family responsibilities or do you have family stresses (children with problems, aging parents who need care, illness, or recent death of spouse)? Is your retirement voluntary or imposed? Are you in good health? Are there other stresses? For example, if you retire at the same time that your significant other becomes critically ill, coping with retirement becomes doubly difficult.

The issue of timing is critical. If your retirement is at a "good" time in your life, at the time you expected it, it can be easier to deal with than if it is "off-time." The point about "on-time" or "off-time" relates directly to our expectations. Bob did not expect his retirement. For him, it was off-time. David's retirement was on-time because he actually had initiated it.

Barbara's situation enabled her to retire with ease from her position as a nurse. Her children were grown, her retirement was voluntary, and her identity was only partially tied up with her profession.

Self, another critical resource, refers to the personal strength you bring to the transition. Are you resourceful, resilient, flexible, and able to deal with ambiguity? Are you able to use free time, or do you feel more comfortable with a busy schedule? Do you need to set goals? Do you have problems living with pressure?

How tied up in your job is your ego? How would you describe your personality? Are you a happy person? Do you feel depressed? Are you an optimist? Do you move to a new community saying "I'll never make friends," or do you believe it may take time but things will work out? Do you have interests or hobbies you have long yearned to pursue? How have you reacted to the other major lifestyle changes you have experienced?

Jerry, a former science professor, bumped into a brick wall as he tried to create a retirement learning institute at a local university. The administrators set up roadblocks. He felt "ignored and angry." After some time, he began to rely on his inner resources and not take what happened as a reflection on him, but rather as an indication of the narrowness of the institution. His self-confidence ultimately enabled him to create an institute without university backing.

What you possess inwardly clearly influences how you cope. Jan had recently retired and was trying to establish herself as a consultant. She did not do well the week her computer crashed, her cell phone stopped working, and her phone line went dead. She felt unable to deal with the ambiguity of not knowing when everything would get fixed, whether all her work would be lost. For that moment in time, her *Self* as a resource was low.

Supports refer to the external forces that will bolster a retiree during the transition. Are you financially secure, barely solvent, or in debt? Do you have family members and friends who will understand what you are going through? Will they be there to give you the emotional help you may need? How much support did you receive from coworkers at your job, and where can you look for replacements? Are you living in a supportive community? Do you belong to a church or a spiritually oriented group that you can lean on for support?

The support you receive or that is available at the time of transition is critical to your sense of well-being. If a new retiree, for example, moves to a new city, knowing no one, with no supports, the adaptation might be slowed down. If a company closes and provides no support for helping employees secure new jobs, then the newly unemployed are at sea.

Strategies are the specific coping mechanisms you bring to retirement. There are almost always more *Strategies* than people realize. Sociologist Leonard Pearlin tells us that there is no single, magic-bullet coping strategy. The person who copes effectively is someone who can use many strategies flexibly, depending on the *Situation*. On the basis of interviews with 2,300 people between the ages of 18 and 65, Pearlin and Schooler[2] distinguished three types of strategies according to whether you can (1) change your situation by negotiating, taking action, seeking advice, asserting yourself, or brainstorming; (2) change the way you interpret your situation by reframing, relabeling, ignoring, developing rituals, using humor, or having faith; or (3) manage your emotional reactions to the situation by using relaxation skills, expressing emotions, engaging in physical activity, and participating in counseling, therapy, or support groups.

Because Bob could not change his situation he had to change the way he interpreted his situation. He began to reframe it by seeing it as an opportunity to do something new with his life. He relied on his inner resources and had faith that he could work it out. He then managed his emotional reactions by participating in counseling, staying fit physically, and using relaxation skills. However, when it came to dealing with his cancer, he tried to manage his emotions by seeking alternative treatments.

Many new retirees rely on the retirement party as a way to begin coping with retirement. However, the jokes at retirement parties often leave the retiree feeling empty. The movie *About Schmidt* paints an example of the hollowness of the retirement party, followed by the brush-off from his young successor—blows that prompt Schmidt to face his dissatisfaction with his wife, his daughter's choice of a husband, and mostly himself.

Despite the negatives surrounding retirement parties, we know that rituals are important. The late anthropologist Barbara Myerhoff studied how rituals can help people deal with "marginal periods"—when they are shifting from one phase of life to another.[3] Myerhoff suggested that rituals can be meaningful if they are developed with and by the person participating in the transition. One couple, both retiring from the federal government at the same time, announced a transition, not a retirement, party. The focus of all the speeches, including theirs, was on the process of finding a new life, with new opportunities. They acknowledged the losses they would feel and the sadness of leaving colleagues, along with the excitement and fear that accompanied moving into an unknown future. The transition party served as a vehicle for them to express where they were, where they were going, and some of the ambivalence connected with this process.

Your Coping Strategies Worksheet at the end of this chapter uses Pearlin and Schooler's three questions as a way of organizing the many coping strategies available for dealing with overwhelming challenges. As you think about your own situation, you can look at the list on Your Coping Strategies Worksheet and see which ones you are using. Then try to add some new ones, remembering that the person who can cope most effectively is the person who uses lots of strategies flexibly.

Psychologist Richard Lazarus organized coping skills in a very similar way. He distinguishes between problem-solving strategies and those that are emotion-focused. Lazarus suggested that if you have something

119

you can change you use problem-solving strategies; if there is no hope, you manage your emotions with emotion-focused strategies.[4]

A case in point is Terry, former head of a university's physical therapy unit, whose career suddenly ended because of downsizing. He was both shocked and devastated. First he tried to change his situation using problem-solving strategies like negotiating with the university. When that did not work, Terry, a goal-oriented man who thrived on both activity and pressure, gave himself 90 days—it turned out to be 100—to get a new plan in place. During the intervening weeks, he took pains to fill his calendar. Every day he had a project, something to do, to look forward to. If he had two appointments for the week, he would plan them for different days to stretch out the activities.

Terry then used emotion-focused strategies—that is, he dealt with his emotional reactions to his forced retirement. He exercised regularly as a way to manage his emotional reactions to the loss of his job. In addition, he began to tell himself that perhaps this would turn out to be for the best. Maybe the forced retirement would be a catalyst for figuring out what to do with the rest of his life.

So, a word of caution: Beware of catastrophizing! Look at each stressful situation and ask yourself if you can change it. If so, then problem-solve. If not, then change the way you see the situation mentally, reframe it, and try to relax.

The 4 S system can be applied to Bob and David. Bob's *Situation* was complicated by several transitions: leaving a job, searching for a new career, going to school, becoming a therapist, being offered a part-time job, and discovering a major health problem.

Fortunately, he had a strong sense of *Self*. Previously, he went through the major crisis of his life when his wife died and left him with a son to raise. Bob experienced a major bout of depression at that time, for which he sought counseling. Getting through that experience became a source of confidence. "If I coped with that, I can cope with anything" became his motto. In addition, he made a conscious decision that the quality of his life—including having fun— would be a priority. Now that he is facing the challenge of cancer, his strong, positive feelings of *Self* are sustaining him once more.

Also of benefit are the strong emotional *Supports* provided by his second wife, adult children, and grandchildren. When he took the part-time job and moved back into a work setting, community support became available.

In the area of *Strategies*, Bob combined problem-solving strategies with emotion-focused strategies. He took advantage of the job offer at the school to change his feelings of isolation. He used sailing and meditation to reframe his situation. He took advantage of stress reduction methods, sought counseling, and went sailing to regain his inner peace. He also used denial, humor, and work to distract himself and tried to alter his situation by researching possible cancer cures.

To reiterate, if there is hope, you can try to change things. If, on the other hand, you come to the realization that there is no hope—you will neither get back your former job nor get another job—then it is important to concentrate on your emotions. They can lessen your pain by distancing you from the source of the problem and by helping you reappraise and refocus. In other words, though you cannot change the fact of your loss, you can change the way you see it and the way in which you let it affect you.

David's *Situation* also was complicated because he developed a serious health problem, loss of eyesight. However, unlike Bob, David felt defeated. His wife, Dorothy, wrote, "I appreciate David's stamina and determination as I see him deal with his health crisis. Fear of losing eyesight is ever present and he found talking books an unsatisfactory substitute. . . . What he misses most are physical outlets. . . . David cannot do more than mild walks."

Although he had *Support* from his wife and family, what he yearned for was *Support* from former colleagues. He seemed unable to use the coping *Strategies* he had used as a worker. His resources for dealing with retirement were low, partly because of his early experiences during retirement (no paid work), partly because of what he brought to the experience (defeatism), and partly because aging and disability were tipping the balance of resources toward deficits.

David admitted to me that, had he been a different kind of person, other satisfying projects like the ones he ultimately found might have happened earlier. "But," he rationalized, "they are all the more precious now, a reminder that I still have the skills."

Over time, David was able to change from a Retreater to a Continuer by using more coping strategies, including a sense of humor, albeit self-deprecating. When I wrote back to say he would be a good example in this book of how someone can take advantage of opportunities, and even push for new ones, his reply was "Don't make a hero out of me!"

In a nutshell, taking stock of your resources requires that you identify your 4 S's to (a) see which ones will serve as strong resources for you and (b) focus on those which will impede the ease with which you will negotiate your transition. For example, imagine that you won a raffle. The prize was a mobile home in a lovely Arizona community. That could probably be evaluated as positive. However, because you have temporary custody of your grandchildren, you cannot move from Erie, Pennsylvania. So, your *Situation* of becoming a parent substitute when you expected to be a retiree would be negative resource; there would be no *Supports* in Arizona. This could well determine your course of action—turning down the mobile home and the move to Arizona.

You will see at the end of this chapter how you can rate your resources for coping with your retirement transitions. You will identify your strengths and also the areas in which you need to turn a negative resource into a positive one.

Thus far, we have seen that the Transition Model helps us understand the degree to which our life has been altered—in *roles, relationships, routines,* and *assumptions*—where we are in the transition process, and what resources we bring to the transition, such as our *Situation* assessment, *Self* esteem, *Supports,* and *Strategies.*

How do you use this information? You use it by *taking charge.*

TAKING CHARGE:
MAKING RETIREMENT WORK FOR YOU

The 4 S System can help you make the decision about when to retire. Sally loved her job, despite being overworked. She began feeling that maybe she should retire while she was still young enough to start on a new path. She struggled with this decision for several years. She used the 4 S System as a tool to help her make this decision.

First she evaluated her *Situation.* If she were going to change gears, this was the time to do it. She and her husband were in good health, their mortgage was all paid off, and she had a good deal of energy to work on new projects.

She had financial and emotional *Support,* despite the fluctuating market. Her husband had no intention of retiring, assuring them of a continued reasonable living standard. She had many friends of all ages, some of whom were retired. She had many interests—traveling, writing, and photography.

As for her *Self*, Sally is an optimist. She tends to get overwhelmed because of her perfectionist tendencies, but she is basically healthy and full of humor. Sally uses lots of coping strategies. Most important, she initiates social and professional activities. She knows that she will develop some projects that will engage her, although the specifics are unclear.

Sally reviewed her 4 S's and decided she had everything to gain and nothing to lose. Her decision to retire was a considered one.

On the other hand, Lillian, Sally's colleague, decided not to retire. She lives alone, has limited financial resources, very few outside interests, loves her work, and cannot imagine a life without the work and office. However, Lillian realizes that someday she will have to retire. She has began looking at ways to develop her *Supports* and *Strategies* so that she will be prepared with a project, enough money, and ways to structure a life without work.

The 4 S System provides you with a way to examine your resources, identify your deficits, and make an informed decision.

After you identify resources that are not working for you, ask yourself: Is there any chance this can be changed? Jeff was anticipating retirement by starting a computer business he could conduct from his home. While in the process of lining up accounts, a family tragedy hit: His spouse became disabled. Naturally, he was terribly upset by his wife's plight. But he knew he could not give in to wasting time by asking and contemplating, "Why us?" Although at times it seemed overwhelming, he pushed forward, planning for her care while working hard so that the new business would bring in enough money to insure that her care was the best available. His *Situation* was low, but Jeff was sure he had several resources. He assessed them.

He saw that he had family *Supports:* people who would pitch in whenever necessary and supply shoulders to lean on. Until the new business took off, he had sufficient funds to pay for his wife's home care. Because of his former corporate work and training, he was accustomed to utilizing coping *Strategies* in difficult situations. These, coupled with the fact that he is, generally, an optimistic person, added up to a positive adjustment to the challenges life had handed him.

Barry is a prime example of someone whose resources needed strengthening. A workaholic all his life, he faced the prospect of retirement with dread. Barry's main issue was how to get a life. It would not be easy in his late sixties. He participated in a retirement workshop sponsored by his company. Participants were encouraged to use *Strategies* from each of the categories—changing the situation, changing the meaning of the situation, and managing reactions to stress.

First, Barry was to brainstorm about things that might interest him. Then he was asked to reframe retirement—to try to see it as an opportunity rather than a disaster. Finally, he was encouraged to manage his stress by exercising and learning relaxation techniques.

Barry's wife—with whom he had a contentious relationship from his having put work above everything for so many years—surprised him with a gift of six sessions with a physical trainer. She then suggested marital counseling. Touched by her devotion, which he felt he hardly deserved after neglecting her, he agreed to participate in both exercise and counseling. He wanted to strengthen this *Support* system, which he was shocked to discover he had in the first place! And so, from a situation of just the slightest hope, Barry's life began turning around.

What if you were forced into retirement? You still have choices.

First, can you try to change the *Situation* to get your job back? Can you take some extra training so that you might be rehired? Can you use all your contacts to get another job? Can you get training to qualify you for another job?

Second, can you change the meaning of the job loss? Instead of blaming yourself, can you look at the changing economy and realize you are not alone? Instead of letting yourself get undone, take charge. Redefine this "setback" as an opportunity to move forward.

Third, you can manage your reactions to the stress. Be sure to exercise, meditate, swim, run, or find some other relaxing modality to get you through the time you are working out other *Strategies*.

If, on the other hand, you come to the realization that there is no hope—that you will neither get back your former job nor get another job—then it is important to concentrate on emotion-focused coping strategies.

Let's return to Bob. His *Supports*, *Self*, and *Strategies* are high. In his case, his low resource is his *Situation*—his unanticipated diagnosis of a metastasized cancer. Therefore, the focus is to strengthen his *Situation*. And that is just what Bob is doing. He can refer to Pearlin's coping strategies and ask, "Can I change my situation?" The answer: He cannot change his situation but he can and did change the way he saw it. He is using Lazarus's problem-focused coping by searching for different treatments and learning as much as he can about his particular disease. He, of course, would like to change his *Situation*, but because he cannot do that he is not going to let his *Situation* undo him. He would then ask, "How can I change the meaning of my situation?" He can use Lazarus's emotion-focused coping by trying to reframe the situation and see that his life is a long, positive one and that there are some positives embedded in the apparent negative of having a disease. (Actually, half-jokingly, he pointed out that at least he knew what he might die of!) He can also ask, "How can I manage my reactions to the complexity of my transitions?" To do that, he is relaxing through meditation, sailing, and massage. In fact, Bob just completed another sailing trip across the Atlantic, a voyage lasting 25 days. When he arrived, he e-mailed friends: "For me the adventure will remain as one of the highest experiences of my life. These are the things we do to keep the juices running fresh throughout life."

At first, retirement, for David, seemed to exceed his resources for coping. He retreated. Yet, David later found that he had more choices than he used. When I asked him to describe how he moved into more activities, he explained that "Like all else in my life, I fell into things and not because I planned it." He said that chance led to his connection to the Low Vision Information Center and to placing articles in the press. When I tried to give David credit for his role, he backed away. Yet, somehow, he managed to take one of his low resources, *Self,* and strengthen it.

He could not change his diminished eyesight but he could increase his *Self* and *Strategies* by redefining his situation. He could also, through help from a counselor, begin to deal with his feelings of betrayal, marginality, and depression.

To restate, by continuing to follow several case histories, we have seen how the people involved used the methods recommended in this chapter to turn initial frustration and bewilderment into a satisfying, even fulfilling, way of life.

Transition Tips

☞ **Tip 1. Use the Transition Framework to answer your retirement questions.** Prospective retirees and those retired have many questions: To move or not to move? How to find my niche? How to deal with being underwhelmed? How to feel a sense of identity? How to make this time of life meaningful? How to adjust to the changing relationships in one's life? How to deal with income and possibly health changes? Of course, many other questions infiltrate retirement. By applying the Transition Framework, with its 4 S system, you can take charge of your retirement.

☞ **Tip 2. Make the 4 S system yours.** The key to finding your true path in retirement is knowing the resources available to you—your *Situation*, *Supports*, and *Self*, and then use your *Strategies* to the utmost. Once you identify a lack in a resource, you can ask three questions: Can I shore up the resource? Can I change the meaning of it? Can I manage my reactions to it? For example, if I am in a new town, with no supports, what can I do to change that? How can I meet people and orchestrate a support system for myself? If, for some reason, that is not possible, then I need to change the way I see it. I can tell myself, "You can live without supports for now and use the phone to call people in the place you used to live." You can tell yourself, "This is not forever, and someday I will develop new sets of friends." And last, you can do the things that will help you manage your reactions to the stress of no support. You can pray, seek counseling, and exercise.

☞ **Tip 3. Become familiar with the components of any transition.** Knowledge is power. Remember (1) that your reactions to retirement will change; (2) that your stress level will depend on the degree to which your roles, relationships, routines, and assumptions are altered; (3) that your adjustment will depend on your resources— your *Situation*, *Supports*, *Self*, and *Strategies*; and (4) that you can strengthen your low resources and take charge of your retirement.

☞ **Tip 4. Practice increasing your coping strategies.** Leonard Pearlin continually pointed out in his research that the person who copes creatively is the person who uses lots of strategies flexibly, depending on the situation. Always look at your situation, and then think of new ways to go.

YOUR RESOURCE AUDIT

1. **Rate your resources for coping with retirement.** Think about the resources available to you in each category and list them in the appropriate square. For example, if you feel you are an optimistic, outgoing person who makes friends easily, you could list that as a positive resource under "Self."

	Positive Resource	Neutral Resource	Negative Resource
Your Situation			
Your Supports			
Your Self			
Your Strategies			

2. **Circle the resources you need to work on to make retirement the time of your life.**
   a. Your Situation
   b. Your Supports
   c. Your Self
   d. Your Strategies

3. **Strengthen your resources.** Take a resource that needs strengthening. Look at the Coping Strategies Worksheet on the next page and ask yourself, "Can I change the resource? Can I change the meaning of it? Can I manage my reactions to it?"

Your Coping Strategies Worksheet

Can I change the situation? If so, try:	Now using:	Could use:
Negotiating		
Taking action (including legal)		
Seeking advice		
Asserting oneself		
Brainstorming		
Other		
Can I change the meaning? If so, try:		
Relabeling or reframing		
Rearranging priorities		
Selectively ignoring		
Rehearsing mentally for your future		
Making positive comparisons		
Developing rituals		
Having faith		
Using humor		
Other		

(continued)

Your Coping Strategies Worksheet, *continued*

Can I manage my reactions? If so, try:		
Using relaxation skills; playing		
Expressing emotions		
Engaging in physical activity		
Participating in counseling and therapy		
Joining support groups		
Reading		
Other		

Note. From *Overwhelmed: Coping With Life's Ups and Downs* (pp. 88–89), by N. K. Schlossberg, 1989, Lanham, MD: Lexington Books. Copyright 1989 by Lexington Books. Reprinted with permission.

All this will help you keep retirement in perspective. When lining up coping strategies, recall how you have used them all your life in one form or other. Try to think of this as one more path you are going to travel. Have faith in your ability to take charge of your life and to come shining through this time, too.

6

Learning Retirement Lessons

Handling this new phase of life often feels like reinventing the wheel. Although videos, courses, and books abound on all sorts of life subjects—how to select the right mate, raise children, stay married, cope with divorce or widowhood, keep fit while aging—there have been virtually none to deal with the psychological aspects of retirement. We have literally hundreds of books on financial planning. We have long needed books on the psychological issues of retirement.

At a dinner recently, I was seated next to a man who was about to retire from a career in the Navy. "I am going to be 65 and have no hobbies. I cannot imagine what I will do each day. Do you have any ideas?" Just as we need to learn to read so that the world would open before us, this man needed some lessons in retirement literacy. The following lessons are not foolproof, nor should they be followed in a lockstep fashion. They are lessons gained from the research for this book, which can give hope and perspective to those planning to retire, and those retired who are facing some bumps in the road.

LESSON 1: PREPARE FOR
ADVENTURE AND SURPRISE

The world you move into will be filled with surprises, with unexpected turns.

Stan Hinden, a former reporter and author of *How to Retire Happy*, wrote that "much of what has happened to me since I retired has been a surprise. Some . . . positive, some negative."[1] His biggest negative surprise was heart surgery; his biggest positive surprise was a journalism award.

Linda Ellerbee, former television newsperson, has spoken about failure and success. When her husband left her, she had to raise her children alone. She faced further hardship when she was fired from a major network and diagnosed with breast cancer. Now she is cancer free, has a long-term relationship, owns her own television company, and hosts a children's news show. In an inspirational speech she said, "When life looks bleak, when boredom is in the air, sorrow all around, remember that your fortune has not yet been told."

Jane, a union official who dreaded retirement, found many surprises. As a woman alone whose work had been central to her identity, she could not even say the word "retirement." I saw Jane six months after she retired, and she kept reiterating, "I am so surprised!

Life is just wonderful! I love retirement. I love the way I have mellowed. I really think I have changed." First of all, she joined a woman's group, in which the members dealt with retirement issues. Then she had a card made so that she had something to give out when asked. She also joined a club that sponsored many stimulating intellectual activities. Today, she says, she is not frantic if she has no plans for the day or evening. She is much more laid back. Jane is mystified about the changes—mystified and pleased.

Whether or not life turns out as expected, the one thing we know is that it is full of surprises.

LESSON 2: LEARN OPTIMISM

Retirement, like the rest of life, is filled with ups and downs. Adapting to the inevitable and unexpected transitions requires flexibility, what psychologists refer to as *resiliency*. According to the dictionary, resiliency refers to "the power or ability to retreat to the original form . . . after being bent, compressed, or stretched . . . to spring back."

You may begin to ask yourself new questions: What if I am not resilient? What if I do not know how to seek social support? Can I become resilient in the face of losses or if I find I am not on the right path? Can I spring back after feeling overwhelmed or underwhelmed?

These questions bring us to the work of psychologist Martin Seligman,[2] who studied the different ways people react, especially to negative, uncontrollable, or bad events. According to Seligman, those who feel optimistic about their own power to control at least some portions of their lives tend to experience less depression. Optimism, he claimed, is good for your performance, and good for your overall health. Seligman further suggested that the individual's *explanatory style*—the way a person thinks about events or transitions—can explain why some people are able to weather transitions without becoming depressed or giving up. Because much of life is neither bad nor good but a mixture, a person's explanatory style becomes the key to coping. A person with a positive explanatory style is an optimist, whereas one with a negative style is, basically, a pessimist.

If you accept as truth the T-shirts statement that life is all downhill after age 40, you might feel depressed. But if you see the changes each year brings as "challenges," that there always have been positives and negatives throughout your life, and that there are surely pleasant surprises around the corner, your view of aging will be optimistic. In fact, recent studies link optimism to longevity.[3]

Bud exhibited optimism. He voluntarily gave up his driver's license, because he could not see very well. This led to temporary depression. But he, being an optimist, took the bull by the horns. Instead of focusing on what he had lost, he realized how much money he would save on a car and insurance. He projected how these savings would allow him to hire a driver or take a cab. In other words, he could continue his activities.

What, you might ask, can you do if you are a pessimist, if you see aging as negative and filled with more losses than opportunities? Dr. Seligman trains freshmen at the University of Pennsylvania to be optimists. He found that those who receive this training are in better health than those not participating in these sessions. But you can train yourself. In his book *Learned Optimism,* Seligman shows readers how to dispute their negative thoughts. You can argue with yourself. For example, every time you begin to think negatively and hear yourself say "I can't," argue with yourself. Ask yourself what is preventing you from doing what you want. Pretend you were arguing with someone else who kept saying "I can't." What would you tell that person? Then begin to tell it to yourself. This technique is not meant to argue yourself into a falsely optimistic view, but to help you learn to realistically reframe a given event.

LESSON 3: GET INVOLVED, STAY INVOLVED

Erik Erikson, whose model of human development provided the groundwork for understanding the internal tasks people must perform as they move from infancy to old age, underscored the necessity for vital involvement as one ages.[4] According to Erikson, vital involvement means a sense of energy and purpose in "people, materials, and ideas."

Sociologist Morris Rosenberg suggested that satisfaction with retirement relates to a sense of mattering, feeling that you are valued and appreciated by others.[5] If you are involved in meaningful activities or if you have a project that you feel is significant, you will feel that what you are doing matters, even if it is a solitary activity such as cooking, gardening, reading, or writing.

Titles of recent articles in *The New York Times* reflect stories of people in their sixties, seventies, eighties, and nineties involved in life, and feeling they matter: "Ninety Candles and a Second Wind,"[6] "Many Retirees Find It's Time to Go to Work," "The Art of Aging Well," "Optimism's Bright Side: A Healthy Longer Life," "Successful Aging." Often the stories are about the busy calendars of famous women like Brooke Astor, who at age 98 has to keep her schedule on a computer. Or Kitty Carlisle Hart, who, when asked the secret of her youthfulness, responded, "I practice the piano and sing every day for a half an hour. I swim two to three times a week. I get on the scale every day of my life. And I exercise."

Author Carolyn Heilbrun was so concerned about aging that she contemplated committing suicide by the time she would reach age 70.[7] That is, until she reached 70. Then, she retired from Columbia University and found life exciting in many ways. She wrote a biography of Gloria Steinem, a project she had designed before she retired. This organized her time, providing structure and a sense of purpose. Suicide was never given another thought.

I need to make a caveat about involvement. There is no right way to be involved. For some, it might be an active social life; for others, volunteering; for others, paid work, traveling, learning, just "hanging out," or family engagements. Grandchildren become a major focus for many. The avenue is very individual and can change over time.

I have just finished reading a privately published memoir, *A Salute to Life*, by Mickey Kellner Bazelon Knox.[8] It is the story of a woman who is an optimist, who made things happen, who stayed involved. In her seventies, Mickey founded the Sarasota Book Fair and the Children's Reading Festival that became a model for other communities; in her eighties, she found love again and married. With the encouragement of her husband, she wrote her memoir in her late eighties. She is still going strong. She wrote, "I developed a challenging and exciting new project that has given me untold rewards. In a way, this is my message to those who need to 'get going' in their later years, who find themselves alone or in the doldrums. They, too, can find a new life in one form or another."

Lesson 4: Keep Dreaming or "My Time"

All of us have dreams and possibilities. In retirement, we can all look back and think of all the possible paths we might have taken. By tapping into our hopes, fantasies, and regrets we can construct our desired possible self. Retirement offers us the time to think about new ways to develop.[9]

Although about a much younger woman, Teresa's story is instructive. She lied to a blind date, saying she was an interior designer instead of a waitress. She felt badly about lying, but realized that the untruth reflected how she felt about her career. And it also provided information on what she wanted to do: become a designer. However, she felt it was an impossible dream because she was 50 years old and lacked a college education. Then, with encouragement from a career counselor, she overcame her feeling that time was running out. Her counselor pointed out that she had many years ahead of her. Together they figured out ways for Teresa to get an associate of the arts degree, and then transfer to an intensive three-year program in Interior Design. At the time that some of her friends would be retiring, she would be starting a new career.

Consider your regrets and use your retirement years as "My Time." What haven't you done that you wish you had done? Noah Adams, a host of National Public Radio's "All Things Considered," regretted that he had never pursued playing the piano. For his 50th birthday, he bought himself a grand piano and started taking lessons. Several years later he wrote a book about his experience.[10]

Some missed opportunities, however, are not retrievable. For example, I asked a dental hygienist who was planning to retire in the near future if she had ever considered becoming a dentist. Her answer was affirmative; in fact, she had been offered a full scholarship to the University of Maryland's Dental School.

However, her husband did not want her to accept. She had followed his wishes. Past the age when she thinks she could reverse things, she is beginning to regret that she did not follow her own heart.

An example of using "My Time" to make dreams come true is the story of a janitor in the Detroit school system. Over the years, he yearned to be a teacher in a classroom instead of a sweeper of the room. However, he had other dreams: that his daughter become the first person in his family to attend college. He gave up his personal dream to see that his daughter would have no regrets.

The day she graduated from Michigan State University, she handed him a completed application to the College of Education of Wayne State University. He retired as a janitor (he was eligible for retirement), was accepted at Wayne, and later became certified as a special education teacher—the oldest special ed teacher in the system. Today both father and daughter feel fulfilled, and they thank their lucky stars for "My Time."

Never give up the dream of what might be and use your retirement as a time to make your dreams come true.

LESSON 5: BALANCE YOUR PSYCHOLOGICAL PORTFOLIO

The seesaw from overwhelmed to underwhelmed and back to overwhelmed is really about balance in one's life. It is a lifelong issue, one that is also present during the retirement years. In the case of Patti, who had worked as a special education teacher, she retired and became a consultant helping families with their children's special needs. She found herself overwhelmed, spending all her time involved in these families' problems. So she retired again. Now she is searching for a new activity and feeling underwhelmed once more.

I was discussing this issue with a former colleague. We brought up the fact that when we were overwhelmed with busy jobs and raising children, we said no to many offers for speaking and consulting. However, such demand can change. As one retired executive mentioned, you have only a several year shelf life and then you are no longer asked to speak or contribute.

Nadia retired after a long, successful career as journalist, editor, and author. Actually, her retirement had been forced, about 15 years earlier than expected. She had been relocated to New Mexico by a firm that wanted her to handle its house newspaper. But after three days on the job, she realized that she could not work for the head of the company, who had changed her job profile to twice the work, and wanted her to put in at least 15 hours a week overtime. She refused. "If I were just starting out," she said, "maybe I would have. But I had a solid reputation and did not need to prove what I could do, especially to someone so abusive. At this time of life, it was time for me to have a life."

Nadia contacted magazines in the state, and became a sought-after freelance writer. In addition, she taught creative writing, which led to students requesting that she review their manuscripts. In time, she opened a literary agency to aid them in marketing their work.

However, there are rules she sticks to in order to "have a life." Never a morning person, she does not take phone calls before 10 a.m. Holidays and summers are spent traveling or with her adult children and grandchildren. Every day there is time for a walk, laps in the pool, e-mailing, and receiving correspondence from friends around the world. These boundaries keep the balance of Her Time.

LESSON 6: SEIZE OPPORTUNITIES

The conventional wisdom is that planning ahead will provide the opportunities you want. There is no question that anticipating the future is worthwhile. However, for someone who is deeply engaged in a current job, planning ahead may simply not be an option. It is important to resolve the paradox—the need to plan and, for some, the inability to plan.

For Nat, a pilot forced to retire right after his sixtieth birthday, the next steps are not clear. His exciting, totally engrossing work life left no time or mental energy for planning.

What are such people to do? According to psychologist John Krumboltz and his colleagues, you can follow "planned happenstance."[11] This suggests that you can train yourself to be attuned to chance events that suggest new opportunities. For example, Betty, an architect who retired from the Midwest to Annapolis, joined a Smithsonian Institution excursion to the historic district of Laurel, Maryland. She engaged the leader of the trip in a very interesting conversation about historic homes and preservation. The tour leader suggested that the Smithsonian hire Betty to conduct similar tours. She agreed to do it. In other words, Betty really made this happen by seizing upon a "happenstance."

Bert served on an advisory committee of a major organization in his community. Because of increasing medical problems, he had to drop off the committee. Although his mind was better than ever, his mobility was restricted. After several months, it occurred to him that he could still serve in a productive capacity. Because his career had been in marketing, he suggested to the head of the marketing committee that the marketing subcommittee meet at his complex so that he could still be involved. Bert made something happen. And it seemed so simple—keep utilizing people, work around their limitations, but build on their strengths.

The lesson: Whether or not you can plan ahead, you need to always be on the alert for opportunities that will make your retirement, or your projected retirement, more meaningful.

Lesson 7: Acknowledge Your Emotions

The experience of letting go, especially at a time when the future is unknown, can be very unsettling. However, acknowledging your feelings can relieve some of the anxiety. Emotions serve as signals; they are neither bad nor good, but neutral pieces of information. Each person's retirement experiences are unique. We cannot assume, then, that everyone will have the same emotional reaction to retirement. Psychologist Richard Lazarus categorized emotions in a way that can be helpful as you think about your own retirement.[12] The categories are based on what emotions result from

1. a goal being blocked
2. a goal being attained
3. the sense of ambiguity about whether or not the goal has been reached, called "Borderline emotions."

Look at the different emotional reactions exhibited by some of the individuals discussed earlier. Mel, the retired mail carrier whose retirement plans were blocked, felt fearful about his own future, anxious about his granddaughter's future, and angry at his daughter for being unable to "kick the drug habit." Lenny, a former assembly line worker, and his wife experienced continual feelings of joy and happiness as their goals were more than attained. Most interviewees at some times felt joy about their retirement lives and at other times depressed about the life they left.

If you feel let down, even depressed, then it is important to grieve for what you have lost as a first step to moving on. It is important to identify why you are feeling sad. However, if you feel liberated and excited, then enjoy the ebullience, knowing that this up feeling might be followed by some downs.

Delores questioned whether she should have retired from her job before thinking through her next steps. She had rushed into retirement, expecting to adjust. When we talked, 10 months after retirement, she reported feeling sad and low. On the other hand, her husband slid easily into retirement and did not seem to understand her discontent. I said, perhaps she was "grieving." The word resonated. She felt relieved when I explained that it is important to allow oneself time to get over the loss of the old life structure as one is struggling to replace it with a new one. I suggested that she keep a diary of her feelings.

As we discussed in chapter 1, sociologist Helen Rose Fuchs Ebaugh described this in-between period as "the vacuum" in which people feel "in midair" or "ungrounded." It is as though the individual "takes one last glance backward . . . yet . . . isn't really sure . . . what the future holds."[13]

The struggle of emotionally disengaging from the past is complete when you think of yourself in the present. Then, once you let go, it becomes easier to put energy into something new. Choices about what to wear, where to go, what time to rise, how to focus one's energies can create a sense of excitement—even mystery—about what is ahead. It is important, there-fore, to refocus the lens, to persuade yourself that this new set of opportunities can be the beginning of new ventures and new adventures.

LESSON 8: GO WITH THE FLOW, DON'T FIGHT THE UNDERTOW

In Pat Conroy's novel *Beach Music*, a grandmother explains to her granddaughter how to deal with the ocean.[14] If you are caught in a strong undertow, don't fight it. Instead, let yourself go with it, let it take you out to where there is a dead spot. Then you can regroup, get on top of a wave, and ride it to land.

We have seen that each individual faces different tasks in retirement. For some, it is dealing with identity, for others it is with changing relationships or losing a place held for many years. Whether it is money, body, soul, or identity, there are bound to be some trouble spots. It is important to know where your strengths are. Build on them, look at your resources, and use your creativity to make the most of all you've got.

Just remember that this is a *big* transition or series of transitions. It can be the time of one's life with new ventures or a miserable time identified with losses. The good news is that there are ways to achieve a new balance and a new sense of purpose: over time.

LESSON 9: PLAN A—ALWAYS HAVE A PLAN B

Creating a new life is similar to the path taken by Dorothy and her companions in *The Wizard of Oz*. They took wrong turns, but were ready to try another route when necessary.

Of course, everyone's Plan A does not work. In Marshall's case, his Plan A failed miserably. His scenario for retirement—moving from New York to New Mexico—turned into a disaster. He and his wife, May, had packed up their car, sent most of the furniture ahead by truck, and begun the drive to their new home. Mary became increasingly depressed. By the end of the trip, she was so disoriented and distraught she needed hospitalization. When discharged, she was in and out of institutions, on medication, and receiving shock therapy. Marshall's decision to disrupt every aspect of their lives—which for some would have been an exciting challenge—was overwhelming for Mary. And he did not have a Plan B that would ease her pain. Perhaps if Mary had known there was a way out, she might have adjusted to some extent.

One couple retired to a small town in New Hampshire where they restored an old farmhouse. After five years of trying to become part of the community, they realized small town life was not for them. They abandoned their plan and moved back to Minneapolis, their original home.

With the changing economy, Harry and Martha gave up their dream of buying a small house on the water. They will continue to work five years past the time of their expected retirement. This will enable them to save enough money to spend several long weekends and one week in bed and breakfasts on the water. Not perfect, but at least they are planning wisely. They are willing to adopt Plan B hoping that Plan A will be possible later.

LESSON 10: A PLAN B FOR EVERYONE

No matter what your Plan A is, and whether it works out or not, here are two possible Plan Bs for one and all: Trace your family's genealogy or write the story of your life. Telling that story might help you uncover some secret dreams, some unfinished business, and some guidelines for your next steps.

Muriel realized that her story would go untold unless she wrote it. She wrote it for herself, her children, grandchildren, and close friends. She pointed out that dredging up the past was painful but illuminating. She worked for almost two years and produced a wonderful book that tells her story and part of history.

Then there is Malcolm who took a course called "Memoirs." This course turned out to be the most meaningful experience he has had since he retired. He looked forward to the weekly class, to hearing others' stories, and to sharing his own. He was amazed at the intimacy that developed among those taking the class, sharing vulnerabilities and successes.

Tim retired three years ago. What to do with his time? He too took a writing class and is now working full time on his story. He is aware that his story intersects with the history of the airplane industry, and he is engaged in research to make sure the historical context is accurate.

It is important to remember that you do not have to be a professional writer to write. Your story is for family consumption. In other words, you do not have to be a "writer" to write something that your grandchildren and others will find fascinating and meaningful. They won't be judging the writing but will be treasuring the memories and family history that otherwise would be lost.

Each person's motivation for writing differs. For some it is catharsis, for others a legacy. Whatever the reason, the story is a gift—your gift to others. And it also is a meaningful Plan B to have waiting in the wings in case Plan A does not work out.

7

Looking Forward

Remember, a successful retirement is a continuing pro-cess—a process of self-discovery, of reexamining your goals and expectations, and of building on what you have. All of us have opportunities to make the most of our retirement. As a start for crafting your new life, look at . . .

YOUR RETIREMENT GOALS

George E. Vaillant, psychiatrist and director of the Harvard Study of Adult Development, studied three major groups over many decades: 268 Harvard men born in 1920; 456 disadvantaged inner-city men born about 1930; and 90 gifted women born about 1910.[1] Based on this most comprehensive set of studies, he concluded that, whether rich or poor, there are oppor-tunities for growth and joy at every age, including the retirement years.

Retirement *will be* the time of your life, if you can do the following:

1. Replace work colleagues with another network.
2. Rediscover play.
3. Uncover your passion.
4. Continue lifelong learning.

I asked one man to discuss retirement according to this recipe. Phil eagerly volunteered, "This is the best time ever." He explained that he switched his career as a lawyer with a lifestyle that was competitive, even contentious, to a lifestyle that was cooperative and supportive of others. As a lawyer, the structure of his life was in response to clients' needs, court dates, and external pressures. Now after 10 years of retirement—and despite some health problems that include diabetes and heart surgery—he is invested in a life that is "almost perfect." He plays a musical instrument, practices regularly, and has several groups with whom he plays; he takes French lessons and is writing memoir vignettes in French; he works out daily; he lives near grandchildren; and is in love with his wife of 55 years.

In other words, Phil has met Vaillant's criteria for a successful retirement. He developed a new social network, learned to play, has several passions, and continues to learn.

Can you take this seemingly simple recipe and make it work for you? The answer is yes, if you keep in mind . . .

YOUR EXPECTATIONS

If I were to select the most important thing that will determine your retirement satisfaction, it would be the degree to which your expectations meet reality. If your reality is perceived as less than you expected, you will clearly be dissatisfied. On the other hand, if your reality is more than expected, you will be very satisfied.

For prospective retirees, perhaps most important are your expectations about what retirement will bring. One couple moved from Kansas to Arizona two years ago with high expectations about a relaxed, fun, golf-playing retirement. Right after the move, however, the husband had a major heart attack, followed by a stroke, followed by another heart episode. Formerly an active physician, he now stays home most of the time. They are both "heart broken" as they try to make the best of it. As she said, "This is not what either of us expected. Our assumptions have changed drastically."

Michael, another disappointed man, spent hours with his accountant reviewing his financial future. He knew that he had enough money to live in "the style to which I have been accustomed." He never thought about the psychological aspects of retirement. For the first time, his days were unstructured. He did not realize it would take him so long to figure out what to do with his time. He realized that his financial expectations were being met, but his need for recognition was not. In addition, he never thought about the turf issues when both members of the family are in the same space 24 hours a day.

Contrast that with Molly, a single woman who retired from the Midwest to Washington, DC. To her surprise, she found that the reality of retirement far exceeded her expectations. Soon after she moved, friends also moved to DC. She found others she knew in DC, made new friends, and she actually felt more connected than she did in her hometown of 70 years. Molly is delighted with her situation.

Couples we interviewed in a trailer park were more than satisfied. Many had never expected to have two homes—one in their hometown and one for wintering in the south. To have days not working on an assembly line, to have freedom, and to have more than they expected led to great satisfaction.

One CEO had expected to have the same perks he had had before. Although he had just as much money, he had less power and less prominence. As he said, "I still have lots to offer, but no one asks me."

You might ask, "How can I have realistic expectations about my future retirement?" The answer: There is no guarantee that what you expect will be realistic. Sometimes, your expectations will exceed reality; other times, reality will exceed your expectations. One possible strategy you might use is to interview retirees asking them to catalog the many ways that they have been surprised. In addition, you must be prepared for surprises and remember to be ready with Plans A through Z.

We must create options for ourselves and search out networks and organizations that will help us create lives that are meaningful—by trial and error, just as in adolescence. If you find yourself in an unsuitable path, then try another. Finally, you will settle in and create . . .

Your Own Name for Retirement

Jeffrey Sonnenfeld, author of *The Hero's Farewell*, a study of retired CEOs, found that most of those he studied "shuddered" each time the word retirement was applied to them.[2] Ruth, a therapist, suggested that the word implied "boxed in." John refused to use the "R" word after he retired. And the dictionary definition of "retire" doesn't mince words: "To withdraw . . . to retreat . . . to give up one's work."

Contrast all of that with the words of Jeanette, a paralegal in the Justice Department, who said, "I *love* the word retirement. It is a word that reflects control . . . one of the few times when you are in control. You can finally decide for yourself what you want to do." And Fran, who retired after 40 years as an administrative assistant in a large corporation, is thrilled each time she hears the word retirement. It implies time to do the "things you want to do."

Studs Terkel, chronicler of American life, wrote, "To a spot welder at an auto plant, whose daily chore is mind-numbing, retirement after 30 years is devoutly to be wished . . . assuming, of course, an adequate pension."[3]

Sunny Hansen, a recently retired professor from the University of Minnesota reflected about her difficulty in referring to herself as *retired*. Instead, she uses the term *transition*:[4]

> First of all, let me say that I am not retired; I am in transition. I know what I am in transition from, but I do not know what I am in transition to. I do know that my transition has been a planned one—a deliberately chosen, three-year, phased transition.
>
> My insistence on being in transition comes in part, I'm sure, from the stereotypes commonly held about retirement—seemingly negative times characterized by inactivity. But the beginning of my transition has been anything but inactive.
>
> The first year proved to be one of my most active, with continuing international and national speaking engagements (combined with travel); writing articles, chapters, and essays; and attending to editorial reviewing. In addition, I still advise seven doctoral students, and I have an office, phone, and computer in my old building.
>
> It's not quite the same, however. I do feel a sense of loss of identity—like Nancy Schlossberg, I don't know what to put on my business card, so I don't have one. I feel that, with my move out of my office after more than 30 years, something is missing . . .
>
> So far it has been a pleasant surprise. For one who has been so work-oriented, I find that I do not miss the university schedule, meetings, committees, or forms to fill out. . . . I love having time to read the morning paper for as long as I wish. I love having control over my own schedule—it does give me that sense of agency about which we talk in career development—some control, at least, over my time and my life.
>
> So, what am I transitioning to? . . . travel and doing a lot of what we want to do: ski, swim, golf, walk, read,

be with friends . . . more time to spend with my adult children . . . time to think about what I really want to do next—continue writing and speaking in counseling and career development, or trying something totally new.

In an Elderhostel course called "Creative Retirement," the participants suggested words that better reflected their experiences: renaissance, discovery, and rebalancing. They saw retirement as an opportunity to develop your own time structure—being beholden to yourself, not to your boss or the organization. One woman said, "The advantage of retirement is that you can't be fired, you can read the paper and have a second cup of coffee." Everyone in that group agreed that they were "works in progress." Perhaps we should call retirement by another name!

Others have had a similar notion. Daniel Levinson described the tasks of young adults as fashioning their life structure.[5] Going a step further, perhaps retirement is a refashioning of one's life structure.

Alan Fern, Director Emeritus of the National Portrait Gallery, suggested other synonyms for retirement, including the following: "the experienced years, the age of richness, the years of fruition, the time of renewal, or the age of fulfillment."[6] Albert Hunt, of *The Wall Street Journal*, reported that baby boomers are looking at retirement as an opportunity to adventure, start new things, redirect their lives during their "third age."[7] And my editor, Esther Gordon, an author and journalist, suggested one already used in this book, "My Time."

These new words suggest opportunities to continue with what you were doing, adventure into something new, or continue searching for your niche. One woman said, "I had felt unanchored, bouncing around like a ship. I missed solid footing. Now I am experimenting with ways to rebalance my time and my life."

Betty Friedan used the term "adventurous aging" in her book, *The Fountain of Age*.[8] She wrote, "The adventure we are free now to choose in . . . [retirement]—though we can forfeit it or refuse its possibility—may begin with travel or study, but it ultimately involves new ways of work, and new ways of love, that are important not only for our personal survival but also for society—as if, in our third age, which is new for the human race, we are previewing new possibilities for society as a whole."

A colleague in the field of career development, Lisa Avedon, was ferreting out a new way to describe retirement. She ended up looking to the Spanish language. Its word for retirement and pension is *jubilacion*. To retire is *jubilar*, meaning "glee."[9]

Think back to snowy mornings, when you had to get out of your warm bed, perhaps scrape your windshield with freezing hands, and skid to work over icy highways or drive in bumper-to-bumper traffic. It might be that "glee" and "jubilation" are sound suggestions for . . .

Your Future

Are you flunking or will you flunk retirement, or will you pass it with flying colors? The real answer lies in the process.

Here's a quiz to help you zero in on what you need to do to make retirement work for you. Awareness of the process that accompanies any transition can bolster you as you move along through life. Remember, too, if your score is on the low side, you can easily change this. Your score is not permanent. It is simply an indication of what you need to do to make retirement the time of your life. You might just need a little nudge in the right direction to get onto your true path. For, after all, today is not necessarily forever.

YOUR FUTURE QUIZ

Take this quiz to see what you need to do to make retirement work for you. You will get a score from 1 (low) to 3 (high). Remember, if your score is on the low side, you can still do something about it. For each question circle the number that best reflects your feelings, 1 corresponding with the answer "No," 2 with "Somewhat," and 3 with "Yes."

Your Expectations About Retirement

	No	Somewhat	Yes
Do I (did I) have a clear picture of the world of retirement?..................	1	2	3
Am I (was I) aware of the many surprises in store for me?..................	1	2	3

Understanding Your Retirement Transitions

	No	Somewhat	Yes
Am I patient with myself, knowing it takes time to absorb transitions?...	1	2	3
Am I confident that I will be able to (have already) established new roles, routines, relationships, and assumptions?......................................	1	2	3
Do I have strategies to strengthen my resources—my 4 S's?..................	1	2	3
Can I deal with the ambiguity surrounding any transition?..............	1	2	3

Awareness of Your Retirement Issues

	No	Somewhat	Yes
Do I feel I matter despite having no job?	1	2	3
Am I able to handle my financial and health situation?	1	2	3
Without the structure of a job, can I fill my time meaningfully?	1	2	3
Do I have enough friends and contacts?	1	2	3

Satisfaction With Your Retirement Path

	No	Somewhat	Yes
Am I aware that my path will shift over time?	1	2	3
Am I satisfied with my retirement path?	1	2	3

Making Retirement the Time of Your Life

	No	Somewhat	Yes
Do I have dreams still possible to fulfill?	1	2	3
Can I meet—at least halfway—whatever the future brings?	1	2	3
Am I looking forward to retirement, or, if retired, am I embracing it?	1	2	3
To create a happy future, am I willing to spend time reading about retirement and doing some homework on retirement issues?	1	2	3

Now that you have completed the quiz, what can you do?

1. Count the 1's.
2. Think of three things you can do to turn your 1's into 3's.
3. Find a friend or significant other and brainstorm new possibilities.
4. Make several plans and . . .

Remember: Life is not perfect. It never was. The stock market might crash or you might bump into a health obstacle. But as long as there is life, there is hope.

Final Thoughts

The questions, "Now what?" "What's next?" "Am I on my true path?" reflect the need to deal with uncertainty about the future, and the fear of the unknown. These issues are not new. Take the college graduate facing a world with diminished opportunities; the baby boomer facing a world where continuing to work might be a necessity rather than a choice; the new mother concerned about balancing work and family as well as questioning her competency to be a mother; the first time father-in-law wondering how to incorporate this new role in his life; the adult child facing a parent's long-term illness when the family had not been able to afford health insurance; the workaholic person about to retire with no interests or hobbies; and the person pushed into retirement before being ready for it.

The process of dealing with the questions of what to do next in life is similar whether a person is contemplating retirement, or figuring out what to do after high school or college. Only for retirees, this lifelong search is grounded in wisdom and experience.

If you feel overwhelmed about the future, remember you have dealt with transitions all through your life. You already have a modus operandi for dealing with uncertainty. This book offers strategies to hone your skills. It is based on the assumption that your reactions and approach to the future—its uncertainty and surprises—can be under your control. You *cannot* always control what happens, but you *can* control your reactions to what happens, thereby influencing the outcome.

A retired museum director complained that he has the energy and talent to continue successful work, but no one asks him. I recently attended a monthly meeting of a group of retired federal government employees. The purpose: to discuss ways they can continue to be useful and productive. Again, the theme: Will opportunities knock? Many of the participants stated that there are fewer and fewer opportunities as you get older. Some are trying to divest themselves of their work ethic and move into leisure activities. But whether or not they were still trying to stay connected to the work world, this group of executives found that forming a network that provided support for each other is essential in retirement just as in other times of life. Perhaps the former museum director would be helped by such a support group.

Facing any transition—including retirement—raises questions: Am I competent to deal with the future? Who am I now that my past is no longer a prop? Will I still feel I matter to the world? Will I feel marginal, on the sidelines? Do I have hope about the outcome? Will I regain a sense of purpose? Do I feel competent to deal with the surprises of the future? Will I have opportunities to love, be cared for, and care for others?

That is what this book has been about. Yes, there are constraints, yes there are limitations, yes there is age bias, yes, for some, there is a negative label attached to the word retirement *but* YOU still have many opportunities for vital involvement, you still can make a difference, you still can matter.

It's all about passion, an "emotion or feeling . . . of a powerful or compelling nature . . . a strong . . . enthusiasm." Robin Beeman[1] described her novella, *The Lost Art of Desire,* with these words: "The book plays with the idea that desire, the focusing of a passion on an object (or cause) is what keeps artists, and most humans, going. It's something at the core of being truly alive."

This is a time to explore yourself and your world, to rediscover, or uncover, your passion, to stay involved, to create options, and to make the most out of the cards with which you are dealt. The following anecdote about a violinist shows the possibility of turning adversity into opportunity. During the first movement of a symphony, one of the strings on a player's violin broke. To the audience's astonishment, after a brief pause the violinist signaled to the orchestra to continue playing, and they finished the symphony beautifully. When asked about this after the event, the violinist said, "You know, sometimes it's the artist's task to find out how much music you can still make with what you have left."

Notes

CHAPTER 1. DEMYSTIFYING CHANGE

1. Schlossberg, N. K., & Robinson, S. P. (1996). *Going to plan B: How you can cope, regroup, and start your life on a new path*. New York: Simon & Schuster.
2. Ebaugh, H. R. F. (1988). *Becoming an ex: The process of role exit*. Chicago: University of Chicago Press. See pp. 4–5.
3. Levinson, D. J. (1978). *The seasons of a man's life*. New York: Alfred A. Knopf. See pp. 41–42.

CHAPTER 2. LOOKING INWARD

1. Hunt, A. (1999, March 11). Third age elderly begin to give a new definition to retirement. *The Wall Street Journal*, p. A10.
2. Billig, N. (1995). *Growing older and wiser: Coping with expectations, challenges and change in the later years*. Lanham, MD: Lexington Books.
3. Rodin, J., & Timko, C. (1992). Sense of control, aging, and health. In M G. Ory, R. P. Abeles, & D. D. Lipman

(Eds.), *Aging, health, and behavior* (pp. 174–206). Newbury Park, CA: Sage Publications.

4. Rosenberg, M., & McCullough, B. C. (1981). Mattering: Inferred significance to parents and mental health among adolescents. In R. Simmons (Ed.), *Research in community and mental health* (Vol. 2, p. 165). Greenwich, CT: JAI Press.

5. Koenig, H. G., Hays, J. C., & Blazer, D. G. (1977). Modeling the cross sectional relationships between religion, physical health, social support, and depressive symptoms. *American Journal of Geriatric Psychiatry, 5,* 131–143.

6. Gallagher, W. (2000, February 16). Turning from the workaday world to the spirit's concerns. Retirement [Special section]. *The New York Times,* p. 10.

7. Kausler, D. H., & Kausler, B. C. (1996). *The graying of America: An encyclopedia of aging, health, mind, and behavior.* Urbana: University of Illinois Press.

8. Duenwald, M. (2002, May 7). Religion and health: New research revives an old debate. *The New York Times,* p. D5.

9. Moen, P., & Fields, V. (2002). Midcourse in the United States: Does unpaid community participation replace paid work? *Aging International, 27*(3), 21–48.

10. Robinson, J. P., Godbey, G., & Putnam, R. (1997). *Time for life: The surprising ways Americans use their time.* State Park: The Pennsylvania State University Press.

11. Quinn, J. B. (2000, April 3). Planning: The next stage. *Newsweek,* 70.

12. Hoffman, E. (2002). *The retirement catch-up guide.* New York: Newmarket Press.

13. Lazarus, R. S., & Folkman, S. (1984). *Stress, appraisal, and coping.* New York: Springer.

14. Brody, J. E. (2000, July 25). On health report card, the 'F' stands for fat. *The New York Times,* p. D8.

15. Glazer, J. (1996). Too old to work and too young to die. On *Joe Glazer sings labor songs* [CD]. Silver Spring, MD: Collector Records.

Chapter 3. Building Relationships

1. Weiss, R. S. (1974). The provisions of social relations. In Z. Rubin (Ed.), *Doing unto others* (pp. 17–26). Englewood Cliffs, NJ: Prentice-Hall.

2. Kahn, R. L., & Antonucci, T. C. (1980). Convoys over the life course: Attachment, roles, and social support. In P. B. Baltes & O. C. Brim (Eds.), *Life-span development and behavior* (pp. 253–286). New York: Academic Press.

3. Kim, J. E., & Moen, P. (2001). Moving into retirement: Preparation and transitions in late midlife. In M. E. Lachman (Ed.), *Handbook of midlife development* (pp. 487–527). New York: John Wiley & Sons, Inc.

4. Matusow, B. (2000, November). Retirement blues. *The Washingtonian*, 45–54.

5. Sullivan, K., & Jordan, M. (1999, July 13). Japanese retirees fill 'second life' with second jobs. *The Washington Post*, p. A1.

6. Gutmann, D. (1987). *Reclaimed powers: Toward a new psychology of men and women in later life*. New York: Basic Books, Inc. See p. 203.

7. Uchitelle, L. (1997, December 14). She's wound up in a career; he wants to wind down. *The New York Times*, pp. 1, 13.

8. Vinick, B. H., & Ekerdt, D. J. (1991). Retirement: What happens to husband–wife relationships? *Journal of Geriatric Psychiatry, 24*, 1.

9. Pinson-Milburn, N. M., Fabian, E. S., Schlossberg, N. K., & Pyle, M. (1996, July/August). Grandparents raising grandchildren. *Journal of Counseling and Development, 74*, 548–554.

10. Pinson-Milburn, N. M., Hartman, P., & Milburn, G. (1999, September). *Retirement's impact on relationships: A focus group discussion* [Unpublished report]. Frederick, MD.

11. Flaherty, J. (2000, February 16). These trips fill up fast, no matter the destination. Retirement [Special section]. *The New York Times*, p. 20.

12. Glant, D. (2000, February 16). Finding a substitute for office chitchat. Retirement [Special section]. *The New York Times*, p. 20.

13. Jacobs, B., & Schlossberg, N. K. (2001, January 13). *Report of focus group* [Unpublished report]. Holmes Beach, FL.

14. Taylor, S. E., Klein, L. C., Lewis, B. P., Gruenewald, T. L., Gurung, R. A. R., & Updegraff, J. A. (2000). Biobehavioral responses to stress in females: Tend and befriend, not fight or flight. *Psychological Review, 107*, 411–429.

15. TIAA-CREF. (n.d.). *Lifestyles in retirement: New housing choices.* Retrieved March 28, 2003, from http://www.tiaa-cref.org/we_libser/lir/new.html

16. Longino, C. (1995). *Retirement migration in America.* Houston, TX: Vacation Publications.

17. Longino, C. (personal communication, June 25, 2002).

18. Brown, P. L. (2000, August 24). Generation: Raising more than consciousness now. *The New York Times*, p. F1.

19. Hunt, A. (1999, March 11). Third age elderly begin to give a new definition to retirement. *The Wall Street Journal*, p. A10.

CHAPTER 4. DISCOVERING YOUR PATH

1. Moen, P., & Fields, V. (2002). Midcourse in the United States: Does unpaid community participation replace paid work? *Aging International, 27*(3), 21–48.

2. Hinden, S. (1998, June 7). After the big leap, ups and downs. *The Washington Post*, p. H1.

3. Cunninghis, B. (personal communication, April 18, 2002).

Chapter 5. Taking Charge

1. Schlossberg, N. K. (1989). *Overwhelmed: Coping with life's ups and downs.* Lanham, MD: Lexington Books.
2. Pearlin, L. I., & Schooler, C. (1978). The structure of coping. *Journal of Health and Social Behavior, 19,* 2–21.
3. Myerhoff, B. (1984). Rites and signs of ripening and intertwining of ritual, time, and growing older. In D. Kertzer & J. Keitch (Eds.), *Age and anthropological theory.* Ithaca, NY: Cornell University.
4. Lazarus, R. S. (1999). *Stress and emotion: A new synthesis.* New York: Springer.

Chapter 6. Learning Retirement Lessons

1. Hinden, S. (2001). *How to retire happy.* New York: McGraw Hill.
2. Seligman, M. E. P. (1991). *Learned optimism.* New York: Alfred A. Knopf.
3. Duenwald, M. (2002, November 19). Power of positive thinking extends, it seems, to aging. *The New York Times,* p. D1.
4. Erikson, E., Erikson, J., & Kivnick, A. Q. (1986). *Vital involvement in old age.* New York: W. W. Norton & Co. See p. 144.
5. Rosenberg, M., & McCullough, B. C. (1981). Mattering: Inferred significance to parents and mental health among adolescents. In R. Simmons (Ed.), *Research in community and mental health* (Vol. 2, pp. 163–182). Greenwich, CT: JAI Press.
6. Hayt, E. (2000, October 8). Ninety candles and a second wind. *The New York Times,* p. 1.
7. Heilbrun, C. G. (1997). *The last gift of time: Life beyond sixty.* New York: The Dial Press.
8. Knox, M. K. B. (2002). *A salute to life.* K2 Publishing.

9. Markus, H., & Nurius, P. (1986). Possible selves. *American Psychologist, 41*(9), 954–969.

10. Adams, N. (1997). *Piano lessons: Music, love, and true adventures*. New York: Delta.

11. Mitchell, K. E., Levin, A. S., & Krumboltz, J. D. (1999). Planned happenstance: Constructing unexpected career opportunities. *Journal of Counseling and Development, 77,* 115–124.

12. Lazarus, R. S. (1991). *Emotion and adaptation*. Oxford, England: Oxford University Press. See p. 82.

13. Ebaugh, H. R. F. (1988). *Becoming an ex: The process of role exit*. Chicago: The University of Chicago Press. See p. 143.

14. Conroy, P. (1995). *Beach music*. New York: Bantam Books.

CHAPTER 7. LOOKING FORWARD

1. Vaillant, G. E. (2002). *Aging well: Surprising guideposts to a happier life from the landmark Harvard study of adult development*. New York: Little, Brown.

2. Sonnenfeld, J. (1988). *The hero's farewell: What happens when CEOs retire*. New York: Oxford University Press.

3. Terkel. S. (1995). *Coming of age*. New York: The New Press. See p. xxiv.

4. Hansen, S. (2001, March 20). *Reflections on transition, not retirement*. Workshop speech presented at the annual meeting of the American Counseling Association, San Antonio, TX.

5. Levinson, D. J. (1978). *The seasons of a man's life*. New York: Alfred A. Knopf.

6. Fern, A. (personal communication, August 24, 2000).

7. Hunt, A. (1999, March 11). Third age elderly begin to give a new definition to retirement. *The Wall Street Journal*, p. A10.

8. Friedan, B. (1993). *The fountain of age*. New York: Simon & Schuster. See pp. 582, 597.

9. Avedon, L. (personal communication, November, 2001).

Final Thoughts

1. Beeman, R. (personal communication, November 10, 2002).

Index

Activities
  goals for successful retire-
    ment, 154
  "moving in" phase of transi-
    tion, 21–23, 24
  need for balance, 143–145
  pathways of retirement,
    88–89
  pursuing dreams and per-
    sonal goals, 141–143
  sense of being appreciated
    in, 32–33
  sense of purpose and mean-
    ing in, 34–38, 139–141
  time management, 40–42,
    51
  trends among retirees, 87–88
Adventurers, 89, 91–95, 103,
  107
Antonucci, Toni, 58
Assumptions
  changes in retirement, 15–
    16, 110, 111, 112
  expectations for retirement,
    155–157

Attachment relationships, 56
Autobiographical stories,
    151–152
Avedon, Lisa, 160

Beeman, Robin, 167
Billig, Nathan, 30
Boredom, 27
Brody, Jane, 47

Caretaking, 69–71
Change. See Transition
Confidence, 121
Conroy, Pat, 149
Continuers, 88, 89–90, 102–
    103, 108
Continuing education, 40, 74
Coping
  acknowledging emotions,
    147–149
  change in marital relation-
    ship, 61–63, 65–66
  different styles of, 23

Coping, *cont'd*
emotion-focused, 119–120,
122, 128
extent of adjustment, 25
financial evaluation and
management, 45–47
with health situations,
48–50
with loss of spouse, 71–72
optimistic outlook, 137–139
problem-solving skills,
119–120
resource assessment, 114–
124, 130–131, 132–134
strategies, 117–118, 119–
120, 121–122, 131
strengthening available resources for, 124–129,
130–131, 149
transition tips, 50–51
understanding transitions,
109–114
value of friendships, 74–75

Depression, 22, 30
role change and, 30
Divorce, 71–72
Duenwald, Mary, 37–38

Easy gliders, 98–99, 108
Ebaugh, Helen Rose Fuchs,
17–18, 148
Ekerdt, D. J., 66
Elderhostel, 73, 74, 159
Ellerbee, Linda, 136
Emotions
acknowledging, 147–149
emotion-focused coping,
119–120, 122, 128
Enjoyment of life, 22
Erikson, Erik, 139

Expectations, 155–157, 162
family exchange, 68–69, 83
Explanatory style, 138

Fern, Alan, 159
Fields, Vivian, 39, 87
Finances
assessment of resources, 117
choices of living arrangements, 77–82
fear of retiring, 27
preparing for retirement,
42–47, 51, 52
Folkman, Susan, 45–46
Friedan, Betty, 160
Friendship, 73–77, 82
Future quiz, 161–164

Gallagher, Winifred, 37
Gender differences in retire-
ment experience, 59–60,
63–65, 79
Genealogical research, 151
Glazer, Joe, 48
Gordon, Esther, 98–99,
159–160
Grandchildren, 67, 68, 69–70,
71, 72
Grieving, 19–20, 148
Gutmann, David, 64

Hansen, Sunny, 157–159
Hart, Kitty Carlisle, 140
Hartman, Penny, 73
Health
fear of retiring, 27
mental attitude and,
48–50
preparing for retirement,
47–48

social relationships and, 74–75
Heilbrun, Carolyn, 140
Hinden, Stan, 87, 136
Hoffman, Ellen, 43–44
Housing, 77–82, 83
Hunt, A., 27, 159

Identity/self-concept
  assessment of coping resources, 116–117, 119, 121, 130–131, 132–134
  challenges of retirement, 28–30
  identifying pattern of retirement, 102–104, 105, 106–108
  importance of "mattering," 32–34, 50–51
  institutional identification, 31
  period of searching after retirement, 19–21
  retirement audit, 50–51, 52
  satisfaction in retirement, 31–32
  stereotypes of retirement, 30–31
  work and, 3–4, 30
  See also Roles
Internet, 73–74

Jacobs, Barbara, 74
Jubilacion, 160

Kahn, Robert, 58
Kim, Jungmeen E., 59–60
Knox, Mickey Kellner Bazelon, 141

Koenig, Harold, 37, 38
Krumboltz, John, 145–146

Lazarus, Richard, 43–44, 48, 119–120, 147
Levinson, Daniel, 22, 159
Living arrangements, 77–82
Longino, Charles F., 78, 79

Madoka, Yoriko, 50
Marriage, 59–66, 82–83
  loss of spouse, 71–72
Matusow, Barbara, 60
Men's issues. See Gender differences in retirement experience
Milburn, George, 73
Moen, Phyllis, 39, 59–60, 87
Moving in, 21–23, 24
Moving out, 17–19, 23, 24
Moving through, 19–21, 24
Myerhoff, Barbara, 119

National Shared House Resource Center, 79
Nonevent retirement, 14–17, 112–113

Opportunity, 145–146, 166
  retirement as, 159–160
Optimistic outlook, 137–139

Parent–child relationships, 66–69, 72, 83
Paths to successful retirement, 10, 11
  adventurers, 89, 91–95, 103, 107

Paths to successful retirement,
cont'd
  assessment of coping re-
    sources, 114–124, 130–
    131, 132–134
  combination type, 101–102
  continuers, 88, 89–90, 102–
    103, 108
  discussion groups to study,
    104–105
  easy glider approach, 98–
    99, 108
  "moving in" phase, 21–23,
    24
  "moving out" phase, 17–19,
    23
  "moving through" phase,
    19–21, 24
  patterns, 87–89
  phases, 23–24, 24
  process, 15–16, 24
  retreater path, 89, 100–101,
    108
  searchers, 89, 95–98, 107
  self-assessment, 102–104,
    105, 106–108
  understanding transition
    process, 109–114
  unexpected events in,
    136–137
Patience, 20–21, 25
Pearlin, Leonard, 117–118
Physical activity, 47, 51,
  127–128
Pinson-Milburn, Nancy, 73
Play, value of, 154
Preparing for retirement, 6–7,
  17, 34–35
  assessment of coping re-
    sources, 114–124,
    130–131
  backup plans, 150–152
  decision to retire, 124–125

expectation exchange,
  68–69
financial planning, 42–47,
  51, 52
health considerations, 47–
  50, 51, 53
housing arrangements, 77–
  82, 83
identifying pattern of retirement, 102–104
marital relationship, 66
parent–child relationships,
  68–69
psychological issues, 135
self-assessment, 50–51, 52–
  53, 130–131, 161–164
social capital, 39–40, 51, 52
taking advantage of opportunities, 145–146
taking charge, 124–129
Pride, 13, 18

Quinn, Jane Bryant, 42–43

Rejection, 76–77, 96
Relationships
  attachment in, 56
  caretaking issues, 69–71
  challenges in retirement,
    38–39
  changes in retirement, 15,
    16, 110, 111, 112
  changing needs, 55–58
  fear of being lonely in retire-
    ment, 27
  friendships, 73–77
  goals for successful retire-
    ment, 154
  loss of spouse, 71–72
  marital/partner, 59–66, 71–
    72, 82–83

nurturance needs in, 56–57
parent–child, 66–69, 72, 83
preparing for retirement,
39–40, 51, 52, 82
reliable alliance in, 57
self-audit, 84–85
self-worth needs in, 57
social integration in, 56
social support structure,
58–59
as source of guidance,
57–58
workplace as source of social life, 38–39
Resiliency, 137
Resource assessment, 114–
124, 130–131, 132–134
Retirement Audit, 25, 26,
52–53
Retirement communities, 79
Retirement parties, 118
Retreaters, 89, 100–101, 108
Rituals of retirement, 15,
118–119
Robinson, John P., 42
Rodin, Judith, 30
Roles
changes in retirement, 14,
15, 29–30, 110, 111, 112
letting go of past roles,
17–19
See also Self-concept
Rosenberg, Morris, 32, 140
Routines, changes in retirement, 15, 16, 110, 111,
112

Satisfaction in retirement,
49–50
adventurer approach, 91–95
continuer approach, 88,
89–90

criteria for, 153–154
importance of "mattering,"
32–34
meeting expectations,
155–157
self-concept, 31–32
sense of purpose and meaning, 34–38, 139–141
Schedule planning, 40–42
Schooler, C., 117–118
Searchers, 89, 95–98, 107
Self. See Identity/self-concept
Seligman, Martin, 137–138,
139
Shared housing, 79
Situation, 115, 117–118, 123,
124, 127, 128–129
Sloan, Richard, 38
Sonnenfeld, Jeffrey, 157
Spirituality and religion, 36–
38, 51
Stereotypes of retirement,
30–31
Stresses of retirement, 27
caretaking demands, 69–71
changes in social life,
38–40
financial, 42–47
health issues, 47–50
identity and self-concept,
28–32
lack of sense of importance
and meaning in life,
32–37
marital relationship, 60–66
parent–child relationships,
66–69
strained social relationships,
75–77
time management, 40–42
See also Coping
Support system, 117, 121,
122, 124–125, 126, 127

Terkel, Studs, 157
Time management, 40–42, 51
  easy glider approach, 98–99
Timko, Christine, 30
Transitions
  in adult life, 4–5
  challenges of retirement, 9–
    10, 13–14, 165–168
  changes in relationship
    needs, 55–58
  establishing new life struc-
    ture, 21–23, 24
  framework for dealing with,
    109, 130
  as nonevent, 14–15,
    112–113
  period of searching after re-
    tirement, 19–21, 95–98
  process, 109–114, 162
  resources for coping with,
    114–124, 149
  retirement, 157–159
  taking advantage of opportu-
    nities, 145–146
  taking charge, 124–129
  unease about retirement, 5–
    6, 27–28

Travel and tourism, 73
Trial retirement, 66

Unexpected retirement, 14–16

Vaillant, George E., 153
Vinick, B. H., 66
Volunteerism, 56, 87, 88

Weiss, Robert, 55–56
Wet leaves phenomenon, 60
Widowhood, 71–72
Women's issues. *See* Gender
    differences in retirement
    experience
Work
  after retirement, 87–88,
    89–90
  gender differences in retire-
    ment experience, 59–60
  retirement parties, 118
  self-concept and, 3–4, 30
  social life and, 38–39
Writing your story, 151–152

About the Author

Nancy K. Schlossberg, EdD, counseling psychologist, is author of *Overwhelmed: Coping With Life's Ups and Down* and coauthor of *Going to Plan B: How You Can Cope, Regroup, and Start Your Life on a New Path*. She is frequently quoted in the popular press, including *Reader's Digest, Better Homes and Gardens, Lifetime, The New York Times, The Wall Street Journal,* and *USA Today* about mid-life and aging, transitions, and coping. She is copresident of the consulting firm TransitionWorks, Professor Emerita at the University of Maryland, College Park, and has served as president of the National Career Development Association. Dr. Schlossberg has been honored for her work by the American Psychological Association where she is a fellow in three divisions.